Rocks
&
Minerals

Collector's Series

Rocks & Minerals

by Paul E. Desautels

from the collection of the Smithsonian Institution
with photographs by the author

A Ridge Press Book • Grosset & Dunlap Publishers, New York

Editor-in-Chief: Jerry Mason
Editor: Adolph Suehsdorf
Art Director: Albert Squillace
Project Art Director: Harry Brocke
Managing Editor: Moira Duggan
Associate Editor: Mimi Gold
Associate Editor: Barbara Hoffbeck
Associate Editor: Jean Walker
Art Associate: Mark Liebergall
Art Associate: David Namias
Art Production: Doris Mullane

Rocks & Minerals by Paul E. Desautels
Copyright 1974 in all countries of the
International Copyright Union
by The Ridge Press, Inc. and Grosset & Dunlap, Inc.
All rights reserved including
the right of reproduction in whole or in part.
Prepared and produced by The Ridge Press, Inc.
Published in 1974 by Grosset & Dunlap, Inc.
Published simultaneously in Canada.
Library of Congress Catalog Card Number: 73-91134
ISBN: 0-448-11540-9
Printed and bound in Italy
by Mondadori Editore, Verona.

Contents

PART 1: COLLECTIONS 6

PART 2: COLLECTING 146

PART 1: COLLECTIONS

Every great mineral museum in the world is based upon collections made by amateurs who have devoted untold amounts of enthusiasm, time, and money to assembling the buried treasures of the earth. Somehow, treasure is more fascinating to people if it is buried.

The urge to search for buried treasures seems almost universal. Although for most people the whole idea remains only a fantasy, for many it becomes a surprisingly exciting and real pursuit. They are the ones fortunate enough to become collectors, connoisseurs, or students of rocks, minerals, or gems. It is an appropriate activity for people to pursue. Since man is completely dependent for his physical existence on what he can make the earth yield of its life-giving resources, some knowledge of or experience with its natural buried treasures is essential before he can begin to understand his relationship to his planet. The minerals with which he works make up rocks. There is merely a thin film of life, of which he is a part, sparsely spread over a crust of solid rock at the surface of a great sphere of fluid rock. Collecting, appreciating, and studying the minerals is a key to unraveling the fascinating story of the earth itself.

The appeal of the pastime of collecting mineral specimens is based on more than just the thrill of exploration for personal discovery or possession of some mineral treasure. There is something in the hobby for everyone because it can be enjoyed and pursued on any level, from the accumulation of pretty pebbles in a tin can to the abstract calculations of an X-ray crystallographer working on a new-found species. It can be pursued for fun with no scientific knowledge or can absorb the total mental activity of a chemist, physicist, or mathematician for a lifetime.

Perhaps the strongest attraction of the hobby lies in the fact that mineral specimens are highly collectible. Anyone who has the instincts for collecting and appreciating the beauty, perfection, and rarity of objects of any kind can feel perfectly at home with, and highly intrigued by, minerals. In addition, they are generally durable enough to resist the ravages of time, grime, neglect, heat, cold, water, and dust.

A collector may become totally preoccupied with collecting exquisitely beautiful specimens of gorgeous colors and fascinating forms of the sort known only in abstract art. No worry that the entire accumulation is of the same species as long as each specimen is different from the others in some way and has an attraction all its own. He has had the opportunity to build a collection that is an expression of his own taste and appreciation for form and color. Without a doubt, he can be kept forever occupied in locating and acquiring suitable additions to the collection. Once they are acquired, carefully selected pieces can be displayed much as sculptures are exhibited. Fortunately, mineral specimens are available in any size. A hundred-pound specimen of large fans of calcite may be a perfect accent for an interior decoration plan. A group of brilliant jewel-like miniatures may be perfect for the showy living-room vitrine. Many an enthusiast soon finds himself with so many specimens that every surface in sight is covered, or, in self-defense, a series of lighted showcases should be installed to house, protect, and display the lot.

This aesthetic aspect of collecting mineral specimens is a rather new approach for man. Nevertheless, history records, and archeological evidence supports, the story of man's very early aesthetic interest in gems and gemstones, which are, after all, merely selected kinds of mineral specimens. The Bible gives us three major lists of gemstones. Perhaps the best-known is that in Revelations 21:19-20 of the twelve foundation stones, each one carrying the name of an apostle, upon which the New Jerusalem would be built. No ancient religious history is complete without an account of the twelve gemstones in the breastplate of Aaron, the first high priest of Jerusalem. The identification of some of these stones is still not known with certainty, but they include gemstones such as carnelian, rock crystal, lapis-lazuli, citrine, amethyst, and others that are still familiar to us in our own time.

All ancient civilizations prized certain gems. Gem collecting and gem cutting persist today as highly specialized branches of an interest in minerals. More species in greater quantities are available to us than ever before. As hidden treasures of the earth, they are as fascinating now as they were thousands of years ago, perhaps even more, because they are available now to many, rather than only to rulers, royalty, and the wealthy.

Since gemstones are nothing more than selected minerals of rather high durability, beauty, and rarity, they can be treated and studied like other minerals. The fact that they can be cut and polished to plan adds another dimension of satisfying activity for some collectors. Still others may choose to direct their interests toward the art of combining gems with precious metals to produce jewelry and other objects of art.

Aside from the joy of collecting and owning beautiful objects, there can be other kinds of benefits derived from the activity. A collector in Baltimore concentrates on beautiful, high-quality specimens of calcite. By contrast, a "systematic" collector in Rochester is ecstatic when he can add one more new

and distinct species to his collection. There is no collection in the world that contains all known mineral species. Some of the big museums come close to an estimated 1,800 species described in scientific literature. Of this total only a couple of hundred are commonly found, with perhaps a couple of hundred more possible to locate by diligent search. This leaves something like 1,200 as a strong challenge to the collector who wants an outstanding and systematic collection. The remaining 200 are so rare that they will probably elude him.

Setting aside the lure of one species or many, there are collectors to whom the sources are of more interest than the specimens themselves. They study the reasons for the frequent occurrence of certain species as companions in certain types of mineral deposits. Apatite, a species which occurs with wolframite in the ore- and specimen-producing veins of the Portuguese tungsten mines, requires some chemical explanation. Uvarovite, the chromium garnet, is found together in nature with kammererite, the chromium mica—to no one's surprise. But what other chromium mineral species might be expected in the same deposit? The student of these problems of mineral "genesis" soon begins to sort the deposits he knows into a few basic types. With the help of professional papers describing some of these deposits, he can soon become an expert in predicting the species to be found there. Finding one of the buried treasures whose presence his study has already predicted brings him great satisfaction.

Acquiring the ability to distinguish one species from another is a long-term study and may be the only reason for collecting. Many collections are made solely for the purpose of studying the specimens. A collector of this kind probably has more fun and less of a collecting challenge, because the material he needs is easier to find and far less costly to purchase. An odd piece of this species and a lump of that will do. What kind of study he may engage in will depend on personal choice, equipment available, and his experience and background in science. Some collectors have trained themselves to recognize as many as two or three hundred or more species by sight. In the process of developing this skill, a collector will undoubtedly develop an awareness of the workings of the chemical and physical laws of nature in the crust of the earth and may rediscover some of these laws for himself.

Many amateurs, in the course of their collecting, have made contributions to the science of mineralogy. Most frequently this is done by supplying materials necessary for professional mineralogists to do their work. Several species described in the scientific literature have been named for amateurs who found them or who led to their discovery. The insatiable demand for specimens among collectors has also brought about exploitation of mines and other properties that would not be worked commercially. Thus, unanticipated new materials are constantly available for scientific examination.

It is not at all surprising to find that some professional earth scientists, gemologists, and others came to their professions through a beginning in mineral collecting. Study of a collection can easily lead to fascinating aspects of chemistry, physics, geology, and even astronomy. The geologist these days may feel equally at home with rocks ejected from deep within the earth, those found in meteorites flashing in to us from space, and now even rocks from the surface of the moon. However, if the collecting trail does not lead to a profession, it can lead to a lifetime of purposeful, absorbing, and challenging spare-time

activity. Fortunately, doses of activity can be taken in any size to fit the virulence of the collecting disease.

But what of the collector who is inspired primarily by the beauty of color and form? As he begins to develop familiarity with and appreciation for what is available, he soon discovers that many others have trod this path before. There are large numbers of people involved in the hobby. Estimates for the United States have run as high as three million. There are so many hobby clubs and societies—nearly a thousand—that the clubs themselves are organized into great regional federations. The most popular activity of most clubs and federations is the annual mineral and gem show. More or less elaborately staged, the shows sponsor competitive exhibits, and through them collectors are encouraged to exhibit their finest specimens. The competition is keen, and at the larger and more important shows some of the finest specimens in the world outside of museums can be seen. Sometimes even the great museums participate as exhibitors. For show purposes, collectors often work for years to assemble prize-winning exhibit-specimen groups. Of course, mineral-specimen dealers flock to the shows to bring the best of their wares for specimen-hungry hobbyists. Collecting in the United States has become a big enough business that it pays a dealer to work hard at locating fine specimens and making them available.

None of this so far seems very different from antique collecting, stamp collecting, gun collecting, or old-car collecting. The difference, however, is that the rules for distinguishing a very fine from a good specimen, and a good one from a poor one, are largely unwritten. Sometimes the differences are subtle, and they vary from species to species, so that they may be elusive for the beginner. Later such judgments will become automatic, so that more attention can be paid to the realities of specimen pricing. As with most highly collectible objects, the price structure seems to be something that no collector ever feels he has mastered completely.

To become a connoisseur in any kind of collecting is not easy. According to Webster, a connoisseur is "one aesthetically versed in any subject...one competent to act as a critical judge of art, or in a matter of taste." Any amateur can work toward becoming a connoisseur. If he has the time and a strong interest, and if he can develop great patience and perseverance, he is on his way. Eventually, to the extent that his budget allows and that he is able to search them out, his collection becomes rich in specimens of extraordinary beauty, quality, and rarity.

One thing common to all the great connoisseurs of mineral specimens—the builders of great collections—has been a high aesthetic sense. This is an elusive and difficult quality to define. Whoever has it is able to compare specimens and select the best among them. Some collectors never develop the sense. Others suddenly discover that they have always had it.

Even with an aesthetic sense, selecting the best specimen is really a matter of making a judgment of its collecting worth based on a comparison with familiar specimens. One can make such a decision far better if he has already seen and compared many specimens of the same kind, and if he has also heard expert judgment on the subject. Every kind of object has its own standards of beauty and if one is judging minerals the standards of mineral-specimen beauty are applied. A marigold would never win any prizes if judged only by beauty standards used for roses. To judge and select minerals adequately requires the experience of having seen many that are judged best

and many that are judged otherwise.

Because there is considerable overlap in the appreciation of beauty as it occurs in paintings, china, and objects in general—mineral specimens included—aesthetic judgments seem easiest for most of us to make. This explains why so many more collections seem to be based on aesthetically pleasing specimens, rather than on those of scientific significance. Otherwise, the connoisseur-collector would need to become knowledgeable about mineral uses, phases, varieties, relationships to rock, relationships to each other, associations, intergrowths, differences of locality habit, and other scientific data. Of course, even the collector whose interest in specimens is beauty alone must know some basic facts about minerals if he is to collect intelligently. Most of the basic information he needs is in the last section of this book.

One of the best sketches of a mineral-collecting connoisseur is that published of Colonel Louis Vesignié in 1956 by the "Bulletin de la Société Française de Minéralogie et de Cristallographie," which called him a "passionate mineralogist." Translated, it offers a picture of just that. "[Colonel Vesignié's] collection of crystallized minerals is among the most beautiful amateur collections in the world. At an estimate, it contains 40,000 specimens....His collection of precious stones is equally remarkable. It includes a series of pegmatite gems of which certain specimens are exceptional for their size and clarity....He had brought together also a fine collection of meteorites, and he watched for the announcement of new falls to acquire good samples of them....Colonel Vesignié sought after rare specimens, not only to please his eyes and for the satisfaction of being the sole owner of a unique specimen, but also for truly scientific reasons. In fact, from his conversation, it was easy to detect his perfect knowledge of mineral species, their mode of occurrence and association. This knowledge and these aptitudes are reflected in the composition of his collection, where natural series and paragenetic minerals are perfectly represented from the basic species to the rare ones.''

Collections of several of the wealthy, old-time connoisseurs have become the strengths of certain great museums. In the British Museum in London the collections and memories of Sir Hans Sloane, the Right Honorable Charles Greville, R. P. Greg, General N. I. Koksharov, F. N. Ashcroft, Sir Arthur Russell, and others have been preserved. The Smithsonian Institution in Washington, D.C., has its superb collections attributed to Colonel Washington A. Roebling, Frederick Canfield, Professor Dr. Carl Bosch, and others. The Academy of Natural Sciences in Philadelphia houses the great William Vaux collection. Harvard blesses the memory of A. F. Holden, and the American Museum of Natural History in New York that of Clarence Bement and J. Pierpont Morgan.

All of the pieces illustrated and described in this book have been saved from the destructive processes of ore mining and have been reverently preserved, having passed through the hands of one or more knowledgeable connoisseurs. They are all museum-quality pieces with their chances of survival rather bright because of their quality. Although some represent mineral occurrences no longer in existence, a surprising number are still available in the specimen market. They appear in the form of very similar pieces reappearing from private collections and museum exchanges. There are even some whose counterparts are appearing fresh from the active mines of the world. The one unifying feature for all of them is that they represent true mineral-specimen classics. They are among the Rembrandts, van Goghs, and Titians of the mineral kingdom.

Very good mineral specimens are rare among the tons that are produced. Even when specimens are known to be in a mine, the hazards they face even before emerging from the mine are horrendous. More hazards are faced until, perhaps many owners later, they sit safely in an important collection. Most destructive of fine specimens is the shattering effect of the heavy explosives used in mining. If specimens do survive the explosions, most go to the crushing mills anyway. Transportation to civilization, careless handling, improper trimming and cleaning, disrespectful treatment of collections by unknowing heirs, and other hurdles are still to be surmounted. Any one of these can destroy a specimen in an instant. It hardly needs mentioning that large numbers of superb specimens were lost forever through the ravages of World War II in Europe.

The best places to see the old classics are in the important and long-established museum collections. Some old classics and most of the new ones will appear in the exhibits of the better gem and mineral shows. Mineral-specimen dealers also will offer them now and then. Since most dealers were collectors first, you can be sure they will know the differences among specimens and will have them priced accordingly.

It does not follow automatically, however, that high prices mean fine specimens. If not, what are the hallmarks by which they can be recognized? As mentioned before, most of the rules are unwritten but arrived at by common agreement among the knowledgeable. Many years ago, George L. English, the most important American mineral dealer of his time, attempted a set of guidelines for determining specimen value. He included the commercial value of the ore, the mineral's chemical composition, form, rarity, beauty, size, hardness, uniqueness, and minerals associated with it. Certainly, each of these plays a part, but any one of the factors is subject to debate. As things stand, the only sure way of judging is through the experience of talking to those who know and observing the specimens they covet. It is an interesting experience to see three or four real connoisseurs looking over a batch of unique specimens from a new discovery. Without hesitation all will pick out the same piece as being the best without ever having seen the material before. They have learned and are applying some unspoken and unwritten set of criteria.

Obviously, there are some basic criteria anyone can grasp quickly. With few exceptions, any kind of bruising, breaking, scratching, or cracking is lethal to specimen value. Very small blemishes are usually tolerated. Natural discoloration spots or applied coatings and colorings are not acceptable. Dust, grime, mud, and other loose coatings are of no importance because they can be easily washed or lightly scrubbed away. A species that can be brightly metallic should normally be so. If it is a highly colored species, its best specimens are those that exhibit this color. However, if it is always grass-green, a blue-green specimen of the same species may become very desirable. Specimens too large to handle easily and those too small to see easily are least desirable. This is generally true even though some collectors specialize in these unusual sizes. Above all, the specimen's arrangement, or "composition," is crucial. Its parts must be naturally assembled to be aesthetically pleasing, like a sculpture. For example, large crystals scattered over an enormous piece of rock are not so pleasing or interesting as the same size

crystals grouped on a small rock. Also, a specimen with some line, as in a flower arrangement, or perhaps with a strong center of interest, as in a good photograph, is likely to be a good one.

Through experience a mineral connoisseur learns that certain specimens, from old or new mines, have been elevated to eminence, like great works of art, by the judgment of experts. Unfortunately, museum picture catalogues of great mineral specimens, unlike those for art, are seldom published. This means that an aspiring collector of mineral masterpieces must painstakingly make the rounds from museum to museum, collector to collector, show to show. Slowly he will gather together impressions, opinions, and mineral lore to build his own mental reference collection of classics. This book is intended to assist the collector in knowing the classics, as well as to stimulate the appetite of the noncollector. Naturally, then, the discussion of a representative sampling of these classics—the old as well as the dazzling newcomers—is appropriate here.

Minerals for Collectors

NATIVE ELEMENTS: Some elements are found free and uncombined in nature. Gold, silver, and copper occur in the most attractive specimens of all the metal elements. For many years, California has supplied some of the best gold specimens. These vary from large, free-form, stream-tumbled nuggets to brilliant branching groups of crystals. At the California Bureau of Mines in San Francisco are several imposing and weighty clusters of excellent crystals. The Smithsonian has an 82-ounce nugget. The splendid group of flattened crystals in the Cranbrook Institute is also from California, from the Red Ledge Mine.

For silver it seems impossible to surpass the sculptured masses of thick and thin twisted wires and crystal groups from the mines of Kongsberg, Norway. Specimens in the town of Kongsberg itself and in the mineral museum of the University of Copenhagen are world famous. As with many mineral species, however, other mines also produce specimens that nearly rival the best. For silver, the mines of Saxony, Germany, and the Keweenaw Peninsula in Michigan should at least be mentioned. The Michigan mines are also the source of the finest copper specimens. Immovable single masses of copper weighing several hundred tons have been found there. However, collectors treasure more manageable samples with large, well-formed crystals or the sculptural branching forms of very complex or deformed groups of crystals of typical copper color. These branching forms are sometimes so delicate as to simulate the fronds of a fern. Some of the more recently found copper specimens from Ajo, Arizona, are remarkably similar to those from Michigan.

Sulfur and diamond supply the best specimens of the nonmetallic elements. No sulfur-specimen occurrences have yet been found to equal the mines at Agrigento, Cianciana, Racalmuto, and Cattolica in Sicily. Noteworthy for both the size and quality of their yellow crystals, these sulfur specimens often have excellent-quality celestine, calcite, aragonite, and gypsum associated with them. As for diamond, the word seems almost synonymous with Africa, though specimens are found in Russia, Brazil, India, and elsewhere. The great 254-carat crystal in the Smithsonian collection is a well-formed complete crystal and is the largest preserved uncut crystal on record. Smaller but even more perfect crystals are usually available from South Africa, Sierra Leone, and else-where. For the best of them the collector suddenly finds himself in economic competition with the gem-cutting trade.

SULFIDES AND SULFOSALTS: This group of species consists of metals in chemical combination with sulfur. The sulfosalts are similar to sulfides, but have some antimony or arsenic added to the combination. Many of the more spectacular and popular species known are found in this group. In recent times, a flood of superb groups of splendent metallic blades of stibnite, an antimony sulfide, from Baia Sprie, and elsewhere in Rumania, has rekindled an interest created years ago by the discovery of enormous crystals—up to almost two feet—of stibnite from the Japanese island of Shikoku.

In 1972-73 one of the mines of the St. Joseph lead district in Missouri produced, from a large cavity, some of the best galena specimens ever found. A specimen with two joined cubes of brilliant silvery luster, measuring about 6 inches on the edge of a cube and with beautiful light tan calcite crystals nestled between them, is typical. They appeared at a time when much of the old-time quality galena—from the tri-state mining area of Missouri, Oklahoma, Kansas —was disappearing from the specimen market.

No specimen of bournonite, a compound of copper, lead, antimony, and sulfur, has ever been found which surpasses those discovered in the 1860's at the Herodsfoot Mine in Cumberland, England. Resembling brilliant, grayish metallic cogwheels several inches across, the best groups are still in England. No museum can boast the equal of the several that are in the British Museum. Lesser specimens for collectors occasionally turn up from older private collections. Other occurrences in Japan, Rumania, and

Mexico provide fine but less impressive specimens of bournonite.

Good silver-sulfide minerals are constantly in demand and are rather rare, considering the amount of silver mined in the world. Most highly prized are the two "ruby silvers," proustite and pyrargyrite. They are called by the common name "ruby silvers" because they are transparent and red when freshly mined. Unfortunately, if not protected from strong light, they soon undergo a chemical change which blackens them. Proustite in brilliant red, gem-like crystals is best known from the Dolores Mine, Chanarcillo, Chile. In the British Museum there is a crystal over 3 inches long and almost 2 inches thick. Although the Chilean source has long since expired, German silver mines are still producing excellent crystals and groups. Pyrargyrite, the other ruby silver, is known in fine, bright groups of crystals from Andreasberg, in the Harz Mountains, and Freiburg, in Saxony, Germany. Guanajuato, Mexico, and Colquechaca, Bolivia, have produced perhaps even finer specimens.

There are sulfides even redder than the ruby silvers. Two of the best known of these are cinnabar and realgar. Often looking alike, the two species are a cardinal red. Although California is a cinnabar-producing state, its specimens do not compare with the large 2-inch twin crystals from China or the brilliant, pomegranate-seed-like crystals from the mercury mines of Almaden, Spain. Realgar, an arsenic ore, has had a resurgence of popularity like that enjoyed by stibnite. New discoveries of bright-red groups on rock from the Getchell Mine in Nevada and the startling red half-inch crystals scattered on rock from the state of Washington have done it. Cinnabar, like the ruby silvers, tends to darken on exposure to strong light, while realgar alters chemically to the yellow species called orpiment.

Argentite from Germany; millerite from New York; tetrahedrite from England, Germany, and Mexico; pyrite from Elba; pyrrhotite from Mexico; arsenopyrite from Germany and Mexico; chalcocite from England and Connecticut; chalcopyrite from Pennsylvania; and many others from among the sulfides merit inclusion in the connoisseur's list.

HALIDES: The most familiar halide is natural salt. Known as halite, it has been found in many places. Undoubtedly, the finest preserved specimens are those from Galicia, Poland, in the natural history museum in Vienna. There the diameters of the big, transparent cubes are measured in feet rather than inches.

Halite is often avoided by collectors because it suffers from being so soft and is so much effected by changes in humidity. Fluorite, on the other hand, is found in almost every collection. At one time the English lead mines of Weardale and Durham and at Alston Moor, Cleator Moor, and elsewhere produced large quantities of specimens in shades of blue, green, purple, tan, gray, yellow, and amber. So many were put in circulation that it is still possible to find them occasionally in dealer's stocks. The place of English fluorite in collections has been taken over gradually by specimens from the mines in southern Illinois. These are also of excellent quality but do not usually have either the same color range or the gem-like clarity of their English counterparts, nor do they fluoresce under ultraviolet light. Fine, colorless to light-purple crystal groups of fluorite from Naica, Mexico, are becoming highly regarded but are still not plentiful.

Other than fluorite, the most coveted halide

species are atacamite, a copper chloride from Australia, and boleite and cumengite, which are lead-copper-silver chlorides from Baja California. Unfortunately, these are all so rare as to command very high prices whenever a stray specimen or two becomes available. For a short time recently there was a stampede of interest in creedite, when a small supply of good specimens from Mexico was discovered.

OXIDES: Some of the major gem minerals are numbered among the oxides. Here we find corundum—the mineral name for both ruby and sapphire—spinel, and chrysoberyl. Of these gem minerals only chrysoberyl occurs in aesthetically exciting specimens. In Brazil it has been found in beautifully formed, gemmy, cyclic, pinwheel-like twin crystals. Brazil also produces, now and then, crystals of the alexandrite variety of chrysoberyl. Even when not of gem-cutting quality, these are attractive because of the color change exhibited when they are taken for viewing from daylight to artificial light.

Hematite, a common iron ore, is also among the oxides. Common as it may be, some mines yield superb, shiny black specimens for collectors. These vary from the lustrous, rounded masses from Cumberland, England—called kidney ore—to black, splendent crystal groups from Elba and Brazil. Switzerland, from its alpine clefts, has yielded for centuries its delicate but brilliant small rosettes of platy crystals known everywhere as "hematite roses."

Rutile is another common oxide-ore mineral and is the major source of the metal titanium. Although actually a dark-red mineral, it looks black when its crystals become sizable. Synthetic rutile can be made in the laboratory in other colors as well. The best-known natural crystals are the big black-looking lustrous ones from Graves Mountain, Georgia. Although the rutile is usually found there as free single crystals, there are always a few specimens available still attached to the rock matrix in which they grew originally. Shiny black rutile crystals from Mono County, California, are just as good but smaller. Small quantities of rutile specimens from North Carolina have appeared in recent years, looking very much like a network of precisely placed, thick, orange to red needles all at 60-degree angles to each other. The brilliance, color, and pattern of these rutile crystals against the dull brownish rock they are on is a striking contrast.

Cassiterite from Boliva and Bohemia; anatase from Switzerland; cuprite from England, South-West Africa (now Namibia), and Arizona; spinel from New York and New Jersey; franklinite from New Jersey; and many more species give the connoisseur a wide choice from among the oxides.

CARBONATES: If a collector wanted to specialize in one chemical group, carbonates would be an excellent choice. Several species of the group are always available in a variety of spectacular to subtly beautiful colors and forms. There are collectors, for example, who specialize in calcite alone, or in the often paired copper carbonates, azurite and malachite. Many years ago the English mines supplied enormous numbers of excellent calcite specimens which now grace all the major institutional and private collections of the world. With this supply gone, it is fortunate that the gap is filled by different, but very high-quality, calcite in a variety of colors and forms from Santa Eulalia in Chihuahua, Mexico. While the cost of English calcite specimens has risen many fold, those from Mexico are still inexpensive.

The same sort of change has taken place with azurite, a copper carbonate. Bisbee, Arizona, and Chessy, France, at one time supplied the world's collectors with the deep-blue crystals. Now, Chessy azurite specimens are rare and those from Bisbee are increasingly hard to get. Meanwhile, fresh supplies of extraordinary azurite specimens from Tsumeb, South-West Africa, are periodically injected into the collector's market.

A different situation has developed with rhodochrosite, the bright red to pink manganese carbonate. There never has been enough of it to satisfy collectors. A small supply of small crystals from Germany and an old-time supply of excellent crystals up to 1 inch across from Alma, Colorado, were almost the only specimens available. Now, a small new discovery in Colorado of large red crystals and a dribble of very attractive ruby-red crystal groups from Hotazel, South Africa, is just sufficient to keep interest at fever pitch.

Smithsonite, named after Sir James Smithson, who was the founder of the Smithsonian Institution, is a zinc carbonate. The major sources have been Socorro County, New Mexico, with its blue-green "cauliflower" heads of the mineral; Laurium, Greece; and, above all, the Tsumeb and Berg Aukus Mines in South-West Africa. At these mines smithsonite is found in several colors—even pink—and fairly often in unusually large crystals up to 1 inch across. For several years South-West Africa has been supplying the bulk of the good specimens in enough quantity to insure that the turnover from older collections will keep new collectors happy.

Witherite from England and Illinois; malachite from the Congo (now Zaire); cerussite from South-West Africa, New South Wales, and Arizona; siderite from France, England, and Quebec; aragonite from Spain, Morocco, and Sicily; and still more carbonates should be on the collection builder's list.

SILICATES: Most of the world is made of silicate minerals, so that selecting a few outstanding species for mention here can only result in slighting many. Even so, some must be listed. For example, no fine collection can be considered even begun without at least one good specimen of elbaite, one of the tourmaline group.

A recent rediscovery of elbaite near Pala in San Diego County, California, greatly stimulated an already high interest in this gem species. Some of the finest elbaite specimens yet known were recovered there. One of them, now in the Smithsonian, resembles a candelabra with three red and green elbaite "candles" about 2 inches thick and 6 to 8 inches long sitting on end in a row on the rock base. Brazil, too, has steadily supplied its share of elbaite as single crystals or in groups with quartz and other species.

These have been predominantly green, but reddish and two-colored crystals appear now and then. Madagascar (now Malagasy Republic) and Maine are typical of sources adding to the supply. All of these are gem crystals, some suitable for the cut-gem market, but there are also several sources of non-gem tourmaline. The shiny black crystals called "schorl" from Pierrepont, New York, and the large but well-formed brown kind called "dravite" from Australia are among them.

Topaz is another of the gem silicates in much demand. The old-time blue crystals from Russia are practically unobtainable now. However, Brazilian specimens pretty much fill the need, with an occasional assist from southern Rhodesia, South Africa,

Utah, and Mexico. Most of the Brazilian topaz is colorless but in excellent clear crystals. Single crystals weighing several hundred pounds have been found there. The largest of these preserved in the United States is that in the American Museum of Natural History in New York.

The third member of the gem silicate trio that must be included in any serious collection is beryl. Like the other two, tourmaline and topaz, it comes in a series of colors. Best known of these is the blue-green variety with the gem name "emerald." From the dim reaches of time, before the Spanish conquest, Colombia was supplying the best emeralds and it still does. Some of the crystal specimens not of the highest gem-cutting quality make excellent mineral specimens. A year or so ago a rediscovery of emerald crystals in North Carolina brought a new lot of this variety to collectors, most of it being unsuited for cutting purposes.

Beryl may also be colorless, pink, peach, yellow-green, or aqua. The bluish aquamarine gems we see on the market today are cut from heat-treated crystals of beryl that were originally greenish. Green crystals from Brazil are more readily available to collectors than any of the others and they can be had in almost any size or quality depending on how much the collector cares to pay. Pink and peach shades of beryl, known by their gem name "morganite," characterize the beautiful crystals found with elbaite in San Diego County, California, but the same variety is also found in Brazil and Madagascar. However, the bulk of the best beryl specimens of all colors comes from the state of Minas Gerais in Brazil, as do the topaz and tourmaline specimens already mentioned.

Epidote from Alaska and epidote from Aus-tria, ilvaite from Elba and ilvaite from Idaho, datolite from Massachusetts and datolite from New Jersey, danburite from Mexico and danburite from Japan, axinite from France and axinite from California—the world is spanned by classic silicates too numerous to give all their due recognition.

And what about the molybdates, phosphates, arsenates, borates, and other chemical groups? Surely the blocky orange crystals of wulfenite, a lead molybdate from Los Lamentos, Chihuahua, Mexico, must be mentioned, as well as the newer yellow, more lustrous and thinner plates of wulfenite found in Sonora, Mexico. Since the incredible specimens of brownish to yellowish to orange plates of wulfenite from the Glove Mine in Arizona have stopped coming, the Mexican supplies have helped satisfy the insatiable demand for this species, which is dear to collectors' hearts.

Legrandite and adamite, both zinc arsenates, have poured out of Mexico in quantity for several years. There have been enough superb pieces for collectors to trade and sell back and forth to each other and to dealers for many years to come. Fortunately, this is true of at least a dozen more species that might be described here. What it all means is that the Rembrandts and Picassos of mineral collecting are still available and, like new art, new specimens are being constantly discovered among the earth's buried treasures.

The specimens featured on the following pages are selected purposely to leave a strong impression of the subtle qualities that are possessed by all fine mineral specimens. Several are from world-wide classic occurrences, some from what will be the classic occurrences of the future, and all are taken from the collection of the Smithsonian Institution.

COLLECTIONS

Fluorite

Fluorite

The color range of fluorite, due to the presence of impurities and structural defects, is remarkable. Purple, green, blue, yellow, brown, violet, orange, pink, each in various shades, as well as colorless and black are known. It is a common mineral, occurring in numerous deposits from small amounts to thousands of tons. Its popularity with collectors is due to its many colors and its often large and perfect crystals. Frequently, crystals have strong color zonings as well as attractive inclusions of other minerals, such as tiny flashing crystals of marcasite. Fluorite from several English mines is especially desirable because it glows, or fluoresces, a strong mysterious-looking blue when bathed in ultraviolet light in a dark room. Fluorite from other places may have white, tan, reddish, or violet fluorescence or, surprisingly, none at all. ¶ Often fluorite is pure enough to be cut into beautiful gems. Unfortunately, because of its softness and cleavable nature, such gems are only for connoisseur collections and not for jewelry. Although fluorite forms beautiful crystals, the collector must handle it with some care to avoid damage. But, with skill, its cleavability is turned to advantage. It is possible, with carefully directed taps, to cleave a block of fluorite into a perfect octahedron. With some luck, one can develop cleavages in still other directions. ¶ Fluorite, or fluorspar as it is known industrially, is a valuable mineral resource. Its uses are numerous. Used directly as a flux in open-hearth steel furnaces, it helps remove impurities in steel. More exotic uses include it in the manufacture of Teflon and in refrigeration systems. High-purity crystals are ground in laboratories for making special lenses. ¶ Fine fluorite specimens come from so many places that it is difficult to single out the best. However, the English lead mines of Weardale, Alston Moor, Cleator Moor, and Tavistock must be mentioned. The fluorspar mines in the vicinity of Rosiclare and Cave-in-Rock, Illinois, have supplied excellent specimens. For the connoisseur there are the rarer—and more expensive—pink octahedrons from Switzerland.

HARDNESS	4
SPECIFIC GRAVITY	3.18
COLOR	purple, green, blue, yellow, brown, violet, orange, pink, colorless, black
CRYSTALS	isometric: simple cubes often modified; also octahedrons, sometimes twinned; clear to opaque

1.

2.

3.

Pages 18-19: *Fluorite from Puy-de-Dôme, France. 1. Parallel clusters of dark purple crystals from fluorite mining district near Cave-in-Rock, Hardin County, Illinois; 2. A 5-inch elongate cube from the specimen-producing lead-mining district of Cumberland, England, also well known for calcite and barite; 3. A coating of ½-inch, light-green curved crystals from Saint-Jacques d'Ambourg, France; 4. Light-lavender cubes on a spear of celestite from a new occurrence at Muskis, Coahuila, Mexico; 5. Transparent, green, interpenetrating cubes from Weardale, Durham, England.*

4.

5.

Tourmaline

Tourmaline

Tourmaline is a mineral of universal interest. It is valued in the gem trade, coveted by collectors, useful in modern crystal technology, and of special interest to the science of mineralogy. Actually, like garnets and feldspars, it is not a single species but a family of closely related species. Collectors have been inclined to think of it as one species, but the discovery a few years ago of buergerite, a new species, has helped change their attitude. Now species names are coming into common usage, such as schorl for black iron-rich tourmaline, dravite for brown magnesium-rich tourmaline, and elbaite for all other highly colored and chemically complex red, blue, pink, green, and miscellaneously hued crystals. Fundamentally, tourmaline is a silicate of boron and aluminum but is complex because it may have several other elements in variable proportions in its composition. Consequently, it occurs in more colors than perhaps any other family of minerals. ¶ Large crystals from Madagascar are among the best examples of color possibilities. They start with one color at the core and change colors with progressive layers of crystal growth so that in cross section they show a progression of concentric zones in strong contrasting colors. Those known as "watermelon" tourmaline crystals have a red core and an outer covering of green. ¶ Sometimes varietal names, based on color differences, are given to tourmaline and achieve acceptance in the commercial gem trade. Among jewellers, for example, rubellite embraces all red to pink shades, indicolite makes up the blue, and, generally, tourmaline refers to those that are green. Small amounts of good gem-cutting-quality tourmaline are found in scattered and isolated deposits. Most commercial gems, however, are cut from crystals found in Minas Gerais, Brazil. From these mines come gem-like transparent crystals that look like long, thick pencils. They are seldom found attached to rock because the pegmatites in which they occurred have long since been eroded. The crystals are found under rock debris and clay from the decomposition of the feldspar to which they were once attached. ¶ In the United States the best known sources of attractive tourmaline specimens are near Newry, Maine, and in San Diego County, California. Of the two, California has been the more active producer on and off through the years. In the 1970's, large multicolored crystals still attached to their feldspar and quartz matrix were discovered there. Several excellent specimens are already in museums and private collections. A new discovery was made almost simultaneously in Maine.

HARDNESS	7.5
SPECIFIC GRAVITY	3 to 3.3
COLOR	almost any, black most common, green and red best known in the commercial gem trade
CRYSTALS	hexagonal: thick to thin pencils, usually heavy lengthwise striations; transparent, opaque

1.

2.

3.

Pages 22-23: Tourmaline from Santa Rosa Mine, Minas Gerais, Brazil. 1. Black-tipped, transparent, ¾-inch elbaite crystals from Grotto d'Oggi, San Piero, Italy; 2. Strongly grooved and striated, shiny black crystal of schorl from Minas Gerais; 3. Fine, 3-inch deep-pink and green crystal of lithia tourmaline with lepidolite and white albite feldspar from San Diego County, California; 4. Plates of muscovite enclosing a 4-inch spray of needles of black schorl from Branchville, Connecticut; 5. Crystal bursts of schorl on rock surface, from Sierra Blanca, Hudspeth County, Texas.

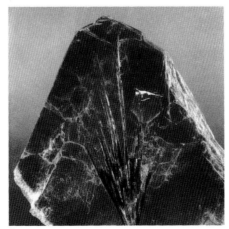

4.

5.

Sulfur

Because it burns readily, sulfur has acquired the ancient nickname "brimstone"—or the stone that burns. In the process of burning, it produces a choking, fumigating gas called sulfur dioxide, which can be further processed to manufacture sulfuric acid. Because sulfuric acid is a necessary chemical for numerous industries, sulfur is extremely important to modern technology. Most sulfur is mined as a free element, although it can be recovered from petroleum and by roasting pyrite, an iron sulfide. ¶ A collector appreciates sulfur for its brilliant color and its very well-formed, transparent to translucent, orthorhombic crystals. The finest specimens of all are found at mines near Agrigento, Sicily, which have produced sulfur since A.D. 1250. Excellent specimens of crystallized white or colorless celestite and aragonite in white to pearly, translucent, hexagonal twin crystals occur with Sicilian sulfur. There are, of course, other minor sources of sulfur specimens; particularly pretty pieces covered with quarter-inch, bright, sparkling yellow crystals come from near San Felipe, Baja California, Mexico. ¶ Unfortunately, sulfur crystals are not too durable. They are so soft that they can be scratched with a fingernail and so brittle that any shock is apt to break them. Even the heat from one's fingers is sufficient to make them expand unevenly, causing cracking that can be heard when they are held close to the ear. In spite of the problems of keeping good specimens of sulfur intact, they add such beauty and high color to a collection that they are worth the effort of preserving.

HARDNESS	1.5 to 2.5
SPECIFIC GRAVITY	2.07
COLOR	yellow
CRYSTALS	orthorhombic: well-formed; transparent, translucent

1.

Pages 26-27: Sulfur from Agrigento, Sicily. 1. Crystals with a thick, gummy, black coating of petroleum, in which they were immersed and which is often found in sulfur deposits, from near Bologna, Italy; 2. A 2-inch, bright yellow crystal with faces revealing its orthorhombic symmetry; 3. Crystals, a dark amber color due to selenium impurities, coated with petroleum, from Racalmuto, Sicily; 4. Bright-yellow transparent crystals up to ½-inch from near San Felipe, Baja California, Mexico; 5. Typical tiny crystals—seen here under microscope—coating a rock surface from San Felipe.

2.

3.

4.

5.

Wulfenite

Wulfenite

Wulfenite The first impression on seeing a good contemporary collection is that of brilliant colors. As the sources of the colors are identified, wulfenite is likely to be seen as a major contributor. Almost gaudy at times, it may be brilliant yellow, red-orange, or some shade of orange-brown. It is one of the few minerals that are almost never formless and massive. It occurs most often in tablets of varying thickness. Some are thin, transparent, and very lustrous. Thicker, brownish tablets, especially those about ¾-inch across, bear a strong resemblance to butterscotch. Crystals measuring over 4 inches on an edge have been found, although they are quite thin and fragile. Wulfenite is a heavy mineral, and specimens are so heavy that individual crystals sometimes cannot bear the weight of the specimen. ¶ Chemically, wulfenite is lead molybdate. It is a secondary mineral derived from the chemical alteration of ore deposits containing galena (lead sulfide) and molybdenite (molybdenum sulfide). Wulfenite has some economic importance; it is a minor source of both lead and molybdenum. Molybdenum metal, when extracted from its ores, is alloyed with steel because it has special steel-hardening characteristics. ¶ Specimens of wulfenite from southwestern United States and northern Mexico have no equal. In Mexico, many exceptionally beautiful specimens have been recovered from the mines at Villa Ahumada, Sierra de Los Lamentos, Chihuahua. They are mostly orange to brown, thick tabular crystals scattered over a white calcite matrix and sometimes dusted with tiny yellow-brown crystals of descloizite. ¶ Two Arizona mines deserve special mention, although many others have supplied excellent specimens. Tabular crystals of a spectacular red-orange color, measuring up to 2 inches on an edge, were found years ago at Red Cloud Mine in Yuma County, and naturally over the years specimens from there have become expensive for the connoisseur. Just a few years ago, at Glove Mine in Santa Cruz County, many were mined from large, open, crystal-lined cavities. Collectors later told tales of having to walk, at the time, cringing with each smashing, crunching footstep, over cavity floors covered with crystals. The predominant colors of these unmatched crystal groups were yellow, tan to yellow-brown, and brown. Many of the crystals were very large. All were lustrous, well formed, and beautiful.

HARDNESS	2.5 to 3
SPECIFIC GRAVITY	6.5 to 7
COLOR	yellow, red-orange to brown
CRYSTALS	tetragonal: thick to thin tablets, usually square in cross section; sometimes transparent

1.

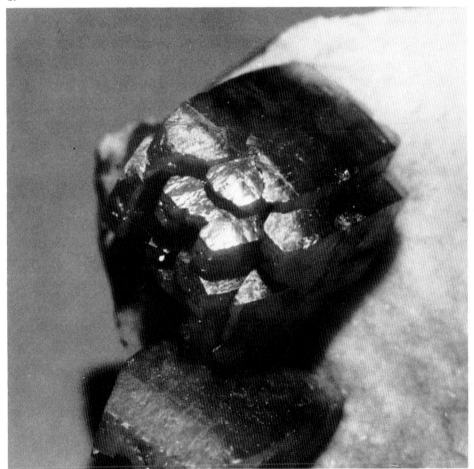

2.

3.

Pages 30-31: Wulfenite from Sierra de Los Lamentos, Chihuahua, Mexico. 1. One-inch, butterscotch-brown, crystal tablets from Sierra de Los Lamentos; 2. Multiple crystal varying from brown to orange at the tips, from the same area; 3. Thin brown tablets with round corners from Glove Mine, Santa Cruz County, Arizona; 4. Clear, amber-yellow tablet about 1/16-inch thick from San Pedro Corralitos, Chihuahua, Mexico; 5. Yellow tablets with disk-like appearance due to many face modifications, from Hilltop Mine, Cochise County, Arizona.

4.

5.

Barite

Barite

Barite, which chemically is barium sulfate, is another species with a very descriptive name. It originates from the Greek word for heavy, and, without doubt, heaviness is an obvious characteristic of the species. Barite is soft and easily powdered, but exceedingly dense. It is ground in enormous quantities to make "heavy mud" for the oil-drilling industry. Used as a filling in drill holes, it helps float the heavy steel shafts and drills to keep them from snapping off of their own weight. Also, the heavy mud helps form a good plug in the holes to keep oil and gas under pressure from blowing out. Of course, there are many other uses for barium, of which barite is the major source, from making whitening in paint to producing heavy, shiny coatings on playing cards. ¶ Not only does barite occur in large deposits but in many places it is found in beautiful crystals. Because of its lack of hardness and its easy cleavage, an undamaged specimen is difficult to acquire. Crystals may be colorless, white, light blue, yellow, brown, or gray. Undoubtedly, the finest specimens for collectors have come from mines in England. They vary from exquisite light-blue glassy crystals from Frizington in Cumberland, to cockscomb-like white crystals from Settlingstones Mine in Northumberland, to the rich dark-brown patterned stalactites of barite from Derbyshire. The United States also has some fine and interesting occurrences. Along Elk Creek in South Dakota transparent and gemmy crystals up to 3 and 4 inches long and of a rich yellow-brown color are found inside rather tough concretions. Groups of flat barite crystals arranged in attractive rosettes are found near Norman, Oklahoma. Locally, they are called barite roses and have a light-brown color and sandy texture due to a high percentage of sand impurities in the crystals. They are different from the small, transparent, light-amber-yellow crystals from the Eagle Mine at Gilman, Colorado, that are sprinkled over rock, like heaps of sparkling gems.

HARDNESS	3 to 3.5
SPECIFIC GRAVITY	4.5
COLOR	pale blue, brown, yellow, gray, white, colorless, other colors due to mineral inclusions
CRYSTALS	orthorhombic: thick to thin, tabular, sometimes rosette aggregates or stalactites

1.

2.

3.

4.

5.

Pages 34-35: Barite from Kisbanya, Rumania. 1. Transparent, tabular crystal partially enclosing stibnite crystals, from Felsobanya, Rumania; 2. Spray of white, partially iron-stained tablets, from Clausthal, Harz Mountains, West Germany; 3. Branching, pale blue crystal cluster from the fluorite mining district near Cave-in-Rock, Hardin County, Illinois; 4. Light blue, thick, pointed tablets from Cumberland, England; 5. Rosettes of crystals, rough-textured and reddish brown due to inclusion of sand, from locality of Norman, Oklahoma.

Rhodochrosite

Rhodochrosite

Two Greek words—*rhodo,* meaning rose, and *chrosis,* meaning coloring—give this mineral species its name and describe it well. It is always some shade of pink, from pale baby-pink, to near red, to pinkish brown. Its color is much like that of rhodonite, which it resembles closely. Rhodonite, however, is a harder manganese silicate, and rhodochrosite is a manganese carbonate. Each species gets its color from the manganese in its composition. ¶ Although occurrences of rhodochrosite are widespread, it does not normally occur in deposits large enough to be an ore of manganese. The common ores of manganese are the black oxides, pyrolusite and psilomelane. And yet, rhodochrosite does, at times, occur in sufficient quantity in copper mines of Butte, Montana, to be an ore. Collectible specimens have also come from Butte, but they are usually pale pink coatings of small crystals. The finest crystallized specimens in the world have come from a group of mines in Colorado. The Mary Murphy Mine in Chaffee County, the John Reed Mine in Lake County, and the Sweet Home Mine in Park County have become familiar names to collectors who appreciate the bright reddish rose rhombs of crystals an inch or more across. In recent times a quantity of excellent lighter pink crystals has come from the Silverton district in San Juan County. ¶ The most noteworthy producer of rhodochrosite specimens, other than Colorado, is Catamarca province in Argentina. There the mineral is mined in large quantities for ornamental purposes. It occurs in thick crusts and large stalactites in lead ore veins. The material is banded in various shades of pink rhodochrosite with contrasting layers of silvery galena and brassy pyrite. Because this rhodochrosite is very compact it can be sawed into slabs and will accept a good polish. Among collectors, cut and polished cross sections of stalactites that show complete concentric bull's-eyes are very popular.

HARDNESS	3.5 to 4
SPECIFIC GRAVITY	3.5
COLOR	pale pink, deep reddish pink, pinkish brown
CRYSTALS	hexagonal: simple rhombs, occasionally scalenohedrons; sometimes transparent

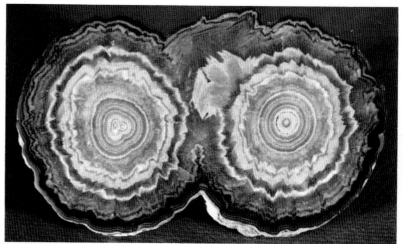

1.

2.

3.

Pages 38-39: *Rhodochrosite from the Silverton district, San Juan County, Colorado.* 1. *Concentric bands of rhodocrosite, galena, and marcasite in polished cross section of stalactites from Catamarca, Argentina;* 2. *A group of simple, bright pink rhombs up to an inch across from the Silverton district;* 3. *Frosty pink, 1½-inch rhombs with white quartz and green fluorite from the Silverton district;* 4. *Stacks of wafer-like, frosty pink crystals with white quartz, from near Horhausen, West Germany;* 5. *Jumbled, paper-thin, brittle, light-pink plates of crystals from the Silverton district.*

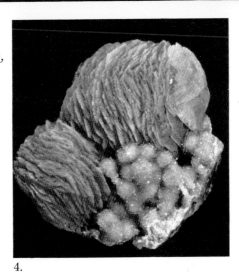

4.

5.

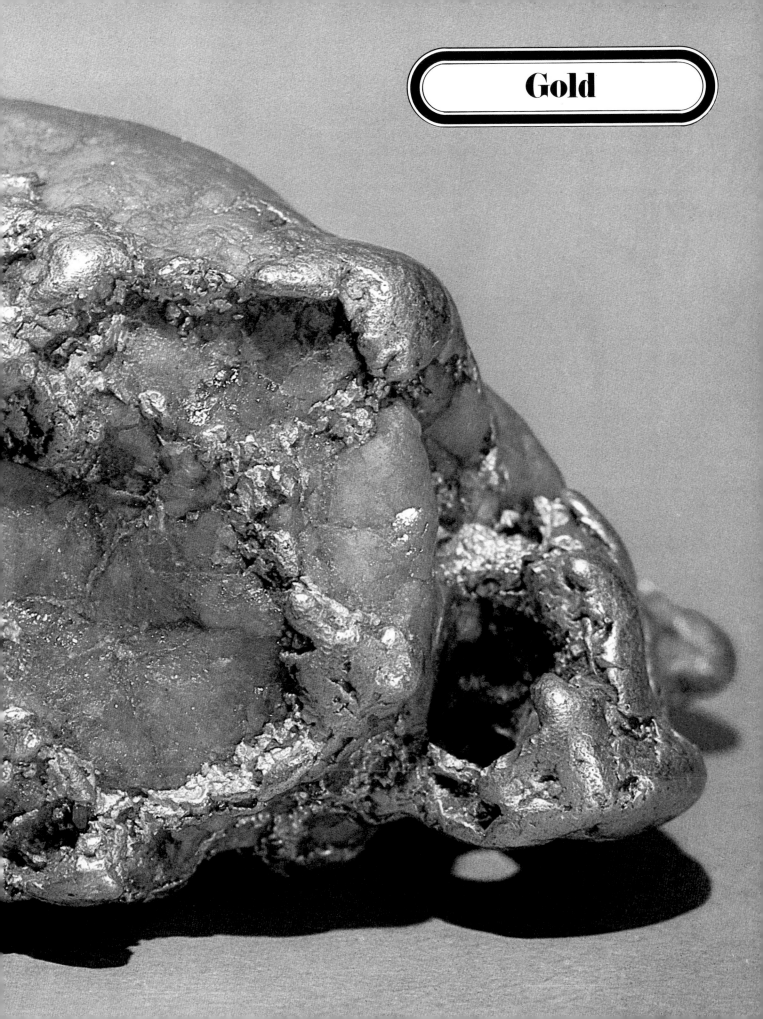

Gold

Gold has been coveted and admired for so many centuries that it is now inextricably entangled with the art, industry, and politics of men and nations. Of the thirteen metals found free in nature, gold has attracted much attention because it is one of the most common. This seemingly strange fact arises from the extreme resistance of gold to even the most vigorous chemical attack. None of the other common metals can exist by itself but is soon attacked, dissolved, and combined with other elements. Iron, on the one hand, exists almost entirely in combination with oxygen. Gold, on the other, is so durable that most that was mined, no matter how long ago, is still in existence in one form or another. ¶ Apart from its monetary worth, gold has many qualities that maintain its popularity. Its color is perhaps the most attractive of all metals. Pure gold, as well as its alloys of higher gold content, is almost totally resistant to tarnish or attack by the normally encountered chemical agents. It is a soft metal, too soft in its pure form to be used for jewelry. It melts and mixes easily, however, with other metals, such as copper and silver, that are able to change its rich yellow color to other desirable hues and to give it hardness without destroying its chemical durability or the ease with which it can be fashioned. The metal and its alloys can be cast, pressed, melted, drawn into wires, and beaten into extraordinarily thin sheets. ¶ Gold that approaches 100 percent, or 24-karat, purity is found in quantity at a number of places around the world. Beautiful specimens for the collector have been recovered from mines in such places as California, Colorado, Rumania, and Australia. Prices established by governments have made it unprofitable, at times, to mine some of the deposits. Now, however, changing gold policy among world governments may once again stimulate gold mining. If so, mineral-specimen collectors can look forward to a new supply of typical octahedral gold crystals, wires, and plates. The California Mother Lode country, a gold-bearing region running for 200 miles along the western slope of the Sierra Nevada, may once more supply nuggets and crystal groups such as those that are now a part of all important mineral collections. Even so, considering the billions of dollars in gold that has been mined in the past couple centuries—more than twenty billion from the Rand District in South Africa alone—surprisingly few specimens for collectors have been preserved. So few, in fact, have been saved that any attractive natural specimen of gold that becomes available will set off a scramble among collectors competing to acquire it.

HARDNESS	3
SPECIFIC GRAVITY	19.3
COLOR	yellow to whitish yellow
CRYSTALS	isometric: octahedrons, dendrites

1.

2.

3.

Pages 42-43: Gold from Spotsylvania County, Virginia. 1. Brilliant crystallized dendrite from the Mother Lode in Grass Valley, California; 2. An interlocking mass of wires, a form in which gold is not often found, from Grass Valley; 3. Curved, deformed, shiny, thick gold leaf from Red Ledge Mine, near Washington, California; 4. Flattened ½-inch crystals recovered years ago from the Massachusetts Lode in Grass Valley; 5. A typical gold nugget, showing rounded and worn surfaces from stream-tumbling in the old gold-rush country of Yukon, Alaska.

4.

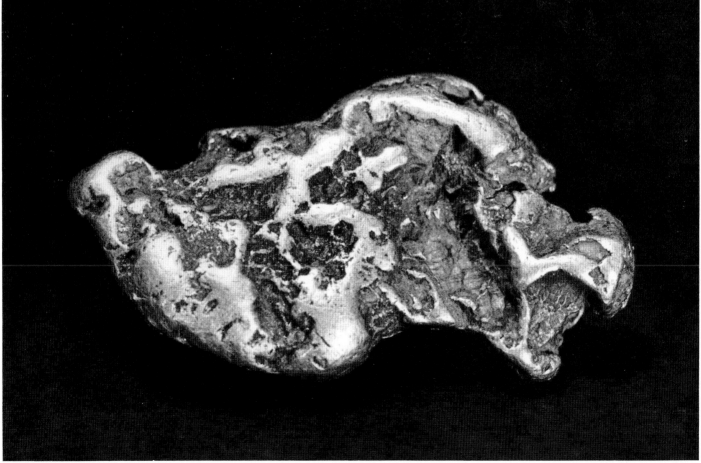

5.

Copper

Copper

Copper is not as good a conductor of electricity as gold and silver, but it is good enough for most purposes and it is available at a fraction of the cost. It is difficult to imagine the crippling effect that a shortage of copper would have on our civilization. Millions of electric motors, with their copper-wound rotors, and untold miles of communication wires would be left unrepaired and unreplaced. ¶ Most of the copper mined today comes from enormous low-grade deposits of other copper minerals, but through the years there has been a scattering of mines producing enough free native copper specimens to excite the collector and to supply the world's mineral collections. Without doubt the most famous of these mines have been those at Coro-Coro, Bolivia; Keweenaw Peninsula in Lake Superior; and Ajo, Arizona. The Lake Superior mines are best known among collectors. They were first used by Indians long before white explorers reached the area. A century-long boom started in the late 1800's with the development of large and productive mines. The largest mass of native copper recovered there measured approximately 44 by 22 by 8 feet. The mines are closed now, but the thousands of beautifully crystallized specimens released while they were active have continued to circulate among collectors. Since there was considerable silver in the deposits, many of the specimens are "half-breeds"—part silver and part copper. Some of the silver specimens are as good as those found anywhere in the world. Approximately seventy other mineral species have been found in the mines, including excellent specimens of datolite, epidote, apophyllite, and prehnite, and superb samples of shiny red copper enclosed in transparent calcite crystals. ¶ Copper is now used primarily for the manufacture of wire and copper chemicals. Alloyed with other metals it increases durability. Copper was used by various early cultures for ornamental and ceremonial objects, and for such tools as knives and fishhooks. These early fabrications, unfortunately, have been poorly treated by time. Copper is subject to chemical attack and, over the years, is badly altered and corroded by weather and soil. Even mined specimens of copper in private collections tend to tarnish and alter, although very slowly, when exposed to moisture and various atmospheric gases. ¶ Among collectors, specimens with well-formed crystals that measure up to an inch or more in diameter, those with branching and often fern-like aggregates, copper wires encrusted with red crystals of cuprite and other specimens—even simple rounded masses from odd occurrences—are popular. Occurrences of odd replacements by copper of hexagonal-looking aragonite or azurite crystals, or other minerals, and inclusions of native copper in calcite widen the specimen choices for a collector to covet.

HARDNESS	2.5 to 3
SPECIFIC GRAVITY	8.95
COLOR	pale red to brown
CRYSTALS	isometric: dodecahedrons, dendrites

1.

2.

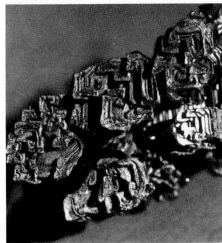

3.

Pages 46-47: Copper from Cornelia Mine, Ajo, Pima County, Arizona. 1. Deformed, fern-like dendrite crystals from Copper Queen Mine, Bisbee, Cochise County, Arizona, the source of many great azurite and malachite specimens; 2. Hexagonal twins of aragonite crystals completely replaced by copper while retaining the shape of aragonite, from Coro-Coro, Bolivia; 3. Unusual skeletal crystals in parallel groupings from New Cornelia Mine, the only large source in recent years of copper specimens for collectors. 4. Stacked, distinct dendrite crystals from Bisbee.

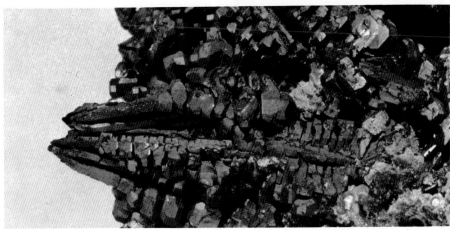

4.

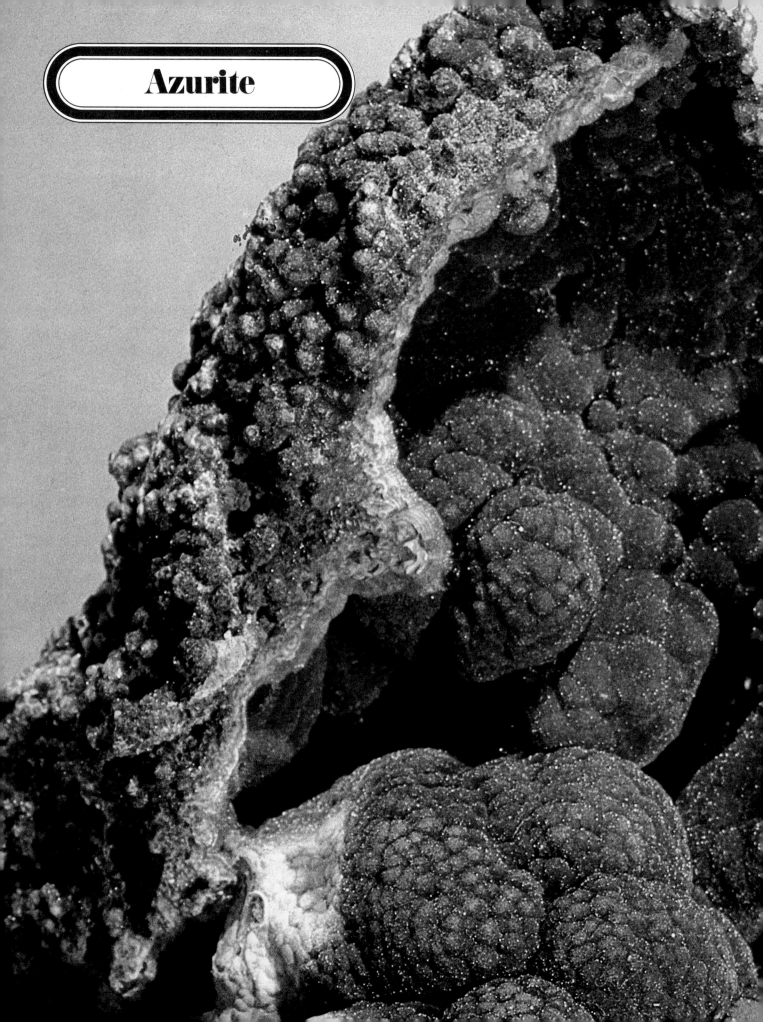

Azurite

Azurite

There was a time when azurite, which has a beautiful vivid blue color when powdered, was used extensively by artists for paint pigment. Unfortunately, azurite has a strong tendency to alter in nature—and in paintings as well—over a period of time with changes in conditions and fluctuations in atmospheric moisture. It alters to bright green malachite, which may make fine mineral specimens—part blue, part green—but is no asset for a painting meant to be blue. ¶ Azurite has much the same origin as malachite —both are copper carbonates—and is a secondary alteration product of black copper sulfides. Being far less abundant, azurite is never found in as great a mass or tonnage as malachite. Rather, it occurs as isolated crystals and groups scattered among other species. Crystals as large as 10 inches long have been recovered from the rich copper deposits at Tsumeb, South-West Africa. Normally, however, azurite crystals tend to be much smaller than that. Usually they are merely coatings or dustings of sparkling blue crystals. The larger they get the blacker they look because the blue is so deep and intense. Large crystals look blue only when light filters through thin edges. By contrast, more finely divided and earthy-looking specimens of azurite tend to be bright powder blue. ¶ Tsumeb, South-West Africa; Chessy, near Lyon, France; and Bisbee, Arizona, are best known for crystallized azurite specimens that have made their way into collections, although there have been numerous other occurrences. Along with the large, well-formed crystals from Tsumeb, 2- to 4-inch rosette-like clusters of deep blue crystals from Bisbee and Chessy are considered particularly desirable. Fortunately for the mineral collector, the meager supply of crystals is not reduced by their use for ornamental purposes. Azurite crystals are not only too soft but also too opaque and dark to be cut and polished.

HARDNESS	3.5 to 4
SPECIFIC GRAVITY	3.8
COLOR	intense blue to nearly black
CRYSTALS	monoclinic: sharp, well-formed, in crusts of small crystals, sometimes powdery or earthy

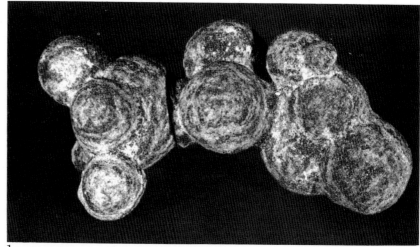

1.

2.

3.

Pages 50-51: Azurite from Copper Queen Mine,
Bisbee, Cochise Country, Arizona.
1. Nodular bright blue concretion containing
sand from Chessy, near Lyon, France;
2. A 2½-inch rosette of shiny, dark blue
crystals found over fifty years ago at
Morenci, Graham County, Arizona; 3. A thick,
bubbly coating of gray-blue azurite, formed
from solutions dripping for years on mine
timber long after work had stopped, from
Copper Queen Mine; 4. Dark blue, shiny,
3-inch crystals from Tsumeb, South-West
Africa, source of the finest and largest
azurite specimens; 5. Smaller but more
brilliant crystals of simpler form from Tsumeb.

4.

5.

Malachite

Malachite

Some of the finest examples of malachite as an ornamental stone have been made in Russia, from a deposit at Nizhni Tagil. They include bowls, vases, and balustrades carved from masses of malachite, tables and walls covered with artfully matched malachite veneers. Striking as it is, in shades of blue-green to almost black-green, malachite is much too soft for most jewelry. Also, pieces of uniformly good quality are too small to make large works of art. This accounts for the extensive use of small pieces of malachite veneer. Because of the persistent demand for malachite as an ornamental stone, it has become quite expensive but is, nevertheless, eagerly sought by mineral collectors who appreciate its color and beauty. ¶ Malachite occurs in nature as a secondary mineral arising from the chemical alteration of black copper sulfides or even of other secondary copper minerals. Examples are the fine red cuprite crystals from Chessy, France, altered on the surface to malachite, and the deep blue azurite crystals, occurring in several places, either partially or completely altered to malachite. Aside from the deposits at Nizhni Tagil, where masses several feet across have been found, malachite has been mined in large quantities in Katanga in the Congo. Chessy, France, and Bisbee, Arizona, are two other noteworthy occurrences. Some of the highly coveted specimens found years ago at the Copper Queen Mine, near Bisbee, are covered with a velvet-like coating of bright green malachite crystals. These are difficult to preserve in their original state because of an almost uncontrollable urge people have to see if the surfaces feel like velvet. They do, but the results from touching are disastrous to the plush surfaces of the specimens. In most places malachite occurs with azurite, its near relative, but far more plentifully. ¶ Seldom does malachite form in good crystals of appreciable size. There are reports of individual crystals up to a half inch in length but they are very rare. Usually the mineral occurs in masses and even in stalactites that show typical concentric layering and banding of light-to-dark green and black.

HARDNESS	3.5 to 4
SPECIFIC GRAVITY	3.6 to 4
COLOR	emerald-green to very dark green, usually banded
CRYSTALS	monoclinic: distinct crystals rare except in very small sizes

Pages 54-55: Malachite from Luiswishi Mine, near Elizabethville, Congo (now Zaire).
1. A 3-inch crystal altered to malachite but retaining azurite shape, from Tsumeb, South-West Africa; 2. Globular masses of malachite formed internally by a series of concentric layers from Copper Queen Mine, Bisbee, Cochise County, Arizona; 3. Sliced and polished colloform mass revealing concentric layers from Clifton, Greenlee County, Arizona; 4. Green stalactitic mass from Copper Queen Mine; 5. Shiny, deep-blue azurite crystal (l.) and azurite altered to malachite from Tsumeb.

1.

2.

3.

4.

5.

Quartz

Quartz is such a common mineral that it could easily lack popularity among collectors. Fortunately, it occurs in such a variety of colors, forms, and disguises, many of which are beautiful, that it is in great demand. The variable conditions under which it forms, the presence of impurities, and the several coloring agents account for the many varieties. Because there are so many kinds of quartz, it is divided into two groups based on crystal size. Crystalline quartz is that with crystals large enough to see without excessive magnification. Cryptocrystalline quartz is composed of aggregates of crystal grains so small that high magnification is necessary. ¶ Among the crystalline varieties, the differences are primarily in color. Rock crystal is colorless, smoky quartz is light or golden brown to gray, amethyst is lavender or purple, citrine is yellow to yellow-brown, and rose quartz is some shade of pink. Of these, amethyst is best known in the jewelry trade, although citrine is often erroneously sold by jewellers as Brazilian topaz. Some of the cryptocrystalline, or fine-grained, varieties are also well known, even among noncollectors. Examples are: chrysoprase, a bright green; bloodstone, a dark green with red blotches; jasper, a brown to reddish brown; and onyx, layered in black and white. Although Mexican onyx is banded in greens, browns, and white, it is really soft limestone and not quartz at all. There are innumerable kinds of cryptocrystalline quartz known as agate that exhibit markings of internal impurities. The beauty of many quartz crystals is enhanced by being laced throughout with needles of rutile (rutilated quartz), flakes of mica (aventurine), or even films of clay (phantoms) that leave an indelible record of the stages of growth. ¶ Because it is so readily available, quartz has many roles in nature. It frequently replaces other substances while retaining their external appearance. At Petrified Forest National Monument there is an entire forest recognizable as trees but completely replaced by quartz of various bright colors. Quartz also often makes natural molds and casts of numerous other minerals. ¶ Because it is such a common species, there are many sources of good specimens. The collector can choose from among the agates of Chihuahua, Mexico, or the rock crystal specimens from the Ouachita Mountains, Arkansas. There is a famous amethyst cave, found years ago in Brazil, that measures about 33 by 6 by 3 feet. Collectors may have to settle today for smaller cavities, such as the quartz-lined geodes, which they affectionately and descriptively call coconuts, from Mexico. The Swiss Alps, today as they have for centuries, supply smoky quartz and rock-crystal singles and groups that are unmatched for their gem-like quality. The supply of quartz specimens from around the world is good and seems endless.

HARDNESS	7	
SPECIFIC GRAVITY	2.7	
COLOR	violet, pink, green, blue, yellow-brown, brown, red-brown, black, gray, colorless	
CRYSTALS	hexagonal: many modified forms, sometimes unusually deformed	

1.

2.

3.

Pages 58-59: Quartz from Galilea, Minas Gerais, Brazil. 1. Quartz casts of cracks in dried mud, made by quartz from solutions filling empty spaces, from Cumberland, England; 2. An 8-inch group of milky crystals with curved faces from near Ouray, Ouray County, Colorado; 3. Scepter crystals with an overgrowth of quartz on the end of another quartz crystal, which occur with surprising frequency, from Goldmeyer Hot Springs, King County, Washington; 4. "Japanese Law" twinning with two flattened crystals set at a fixed angle of nearly 84 degrees, from Otameska, Kai, Japan.

4.

Feldspar

Feldspar

Like garnet, feldspar is not a single mineral species but a large family of species. Unfortunately for the collector, feldspar species have so many characteristics in common that it is difficult to distinguish one from another. The species are often grouped into chemical and structural subdivisions. The two major divisions are the feldspars containing potassium and those containing sodium and calcium, called plagioclase feldspars. ¶ The potassium feldspars include microcline, orthoclase, and sanidine. Of the potassium feldspars, microcline is the most interesting to collectors. Because of the process of its origin in very coarse-grained granite-like rocks, microcline can grow into large, well-formed crystals several feet in diameter. Of all the microcline colors, green crystals of amazonite are the most desirable. The color varies from a pale green to a deep blue-green. Some amazonite crystals from Colorado are topped with an attractive white layer of albite, a plagioclase feldspar, and others are found associated with jet-black smoky quartz crystals. ¶ Although orthoclase crystals are not usually very attractive, there are at least two varieties coveted by collectors. In low-temperature solution-veins in parts of the Swiss Alps, a variety of orthoclase, called adularia, occurs in wedge-shaped crystals that may be as large as 8 or 10 inches across. There is also a rare variety of orthoclase found only near Itrongay, Madagascar. It is yellow and transparent, and pieces are prized for gems. Crystals with good faces are uncommon enough to be expensive. Orthoclase and microcline both form twin crystals, known—after their first-found occurrences—as Carlsbad, Baveno, or Manebach twins. ¶ The plagioclase, or sodium-calcium, feldspars, although common, supply few attractive specimens. There are three or four species, however, that collectors covet. Labradorite is one of them, which, when properly illuminated, exhibits a dazzling display of changing blues, greens, and bronzes. Albite is one of the more aesthetic plagioclase feldspars. Its crystals are dead white and are often well-formed and scattered attractively on their matrix rock. Some of the best come from Brazil. Cleavelandite, a variety of albite, occurs as an attractive openwork jumble of flat crystal plates. Amelia, Virginia, supplies the best.

FELDSPAR	HARDNESS	SPECIFIC GRAVITY	COLOR	CRYSTALS
Orthoclase	6	2.6	white, pink, flesh, brown	monoclinic
Microcline	6	2.6	white, pink, flesh, brown, green	triclinic
Sanidine	6	2.6	white, tan, brown	triclinic
Plagioclase	6	2.6	white, pink, tan, brown	triclinic

1.

2.

3.

4.

5.

6.

Pages 62-63: Amazonite from Florissant
area, Teller County, Colorado. 1. Bright
green amazonite, a microcline, with smoky
quartz from near Pike's Peak, Colorado;
2. Maneback twin crystal of orthoclase
from Crystal Park area, Teller County,
Colorado; 3. Wedge-shaped valencianite
crystals, an orthoclase, from Valencia
Mine, Guanajuato, Mexico; 4. Baveno twin
crystal of orthoclase from Baveno Quarries,
Lago Maggiore, Italy; 5. Bladed
cleavelandite crystals, an albite, from San
Diego County, California; 6. Adularia,
an orthoclase, from the Swiss Alps.

Adamite

Adamite

Some mineral collectors are apt to have a distorted view of the relative rarity of adamite, a zinc arsenate. For many years there has been what appears to be an unending flood of superb adamite specimens from the Ojuela Mines at Mapimi, Durango, Mexico. Adamite is a rare species, and Mapimi is the only place in the world where it occurs in more than minute amounts. Minor occurrences of very small crusts of crystals have been found at Cap Garonne, France, at Laurium, Greece, at Tsumeb, South-West Africa, and in even lesser amounts at a number of other places. Most of these mines supply specimens that are suitable only for collectors of microscopic crystals. ¶ Almost all adamite seen in collections is a vivid shade of yellow-green and, because it is usually attached to a matrix of reddish to brownish iron oxides, color contrast is strong and attractive. Adamite has also been found in other colors, but none so attractive. Color is almost always due to the presence of iron impurities in variable amounts. Absolutely pure adamite is colorless, and, occasionally, colorless or white crystals are found, even at Mapimi where the overwhelming bulk of the crystals is yellow-green. As if their normal color were not sufficient attraction, Mexican adamite specimens also fluoresce, giving off a bright yellowish-green glow when exposed to ultraviolet light. It is this characteristic that makes them look so brilliant when seen in sunlight. The ultraviolet light in sunlight causes some fluorescent color to be added to their normal color. ¶ Adamite is a secondary mineral resulting from the alteration of ores that are rich in both zinc and arsenic. As expected, it occurs with such other related secondary minerals as hemimorphite, a zinc silicate, and smithsonite, a zinc carbonate.

HARDNESS	3.5
SPECIFIC GRAVITY	4.5
COLOR	yellow-green, brownish, yellow, colorless, white, violet
CRYSTALS	orthorhombic: often well-crystallized; small but up to an inch; radiating fan-like groups, spherical buttons of radiating crystals

1.

2.

3.

All of these adamite specimens, and that
on pages 66-67, came from mines near Mapimi,
Durango, Mexico, which, having operated
since the 1500's, are the source of the
finest specimens; most Mexican specimens
are yellow-green and occur in a great variety
of forms. 1. Crystals radiating from
several centers and grouped in wheels; 2. An
almost complete wheel; 3. A sheaf of crystals
radiating from the same center but not in
all directions; 4. A crust composed of an
aggregation of very small crystals;
5. Half-inch spheres of radiating groups of
transparent and distinct crystals.

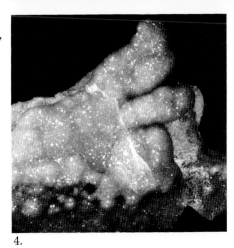
4.

5.

Legrandite

Legrandite

Although traces of it have been found elsewhere, the only quantity occurrence of legrandite has been at the Ojuela Mines, Mapimi, Durango, Mexico. Attractive specimens are found there in cavities in a hard, compact limonite matrix, often associated with adamite. The simultaneous presence of the two zinc arsenates suggests the presence of other related arsenates. Koettigite, an iron arsenate, has been found with legrandite, and very likely others will be found in the future. Nearby, in the same deposits, specimens of other less closely related arsenates, such as carminite, arseniosiderite, and scorodite, have been found. ¶ The deposits at Mapimi, although they contain unusual suites of minerals, are geologically typical of many in northern Mexico. These deposits were originally laid down by hot solutions in highly fractured limestones, replacing some of the limestones and filling in the fractures. Later, the intensive oxidation of arsenopyrite, silver-bearing galena, pyrite, and sphalerite produced close to a hundred different species. Many of them are very interesting mineralogically, and some, such as legrandite, are limited to the Ojuela Mines or are known only as traces elsewhere. Enormous quantities of fine specimens of the various species, including quite a few of legrandite, have found their way into mineral collections. ¶ Some legrandite crystals, especially small ones, are perfectly transparent, and all are yellow. The largest crystals known are between 2½ and 3 inches long, but large crystals tend to be more poorly formed and more opaque, and they are packed in radiating sprays and clusters.

HARDNESS	4.5
SPECIFIC GRAVITY	4
COLOR	yellow
CRYSTALS	monoclinic: usually well-crystallized, up to 3 inches; small crystals are sometimes transparent

1.

All five photographs, including that on pages 70-71, are of legrandite specimens from the Ojuela Mine, Mapimi, Durango, Mexico—the only source of the species. 1. A sprinkling of ¼-inch, transparent, needle-like crystals on limonite, the usual matrix; 2. Single, ⅝-inch, well-formed, transparent crystal, unusual because crystals are almost always found in clusters rather than one alone; 3. An attractive, 2-inch, amber-yellow crystal group with poorly defined crystals; 4. Spray of crystals consisting of opaque but well-formed singles.

2.

3.

4.

Dioptase

Dioptase

Dioptase More than any other single characteristic, color accounts for the popularity of dioptase. In large crystals it is an opaque-to-translucent, deep emerald-green. Small crystals, although a very strong emerald color, tend to be transparent and less intense. Several copper minerals, such as malachite, azurite, and cuprite, each pictured in this book, are highly colored. Dioptase, a copper silicate, is no exception. ¶ Like the other brightly colored copper minerals, dioptase is found in the upper, highly oxidized portions of copper ore deposits. Because copper is plentiful in many parts of the world, and quartz—or silica—is one of the most common species, one would expect that their combination would occur in enormous deposits. However, copper and silica, because of the nature of the atoms involved, have considerable difficulty in combining. Dioptase, as a result, is a very rare species. This is the second characteristic that makes it desirable to collectors. ¶ Although dioptase is rare, there are numerous deposits where it occurs in very small amounts as tiny crystals. There are as few as half a dozen occurrences of interest to the collector. Among them, the now defunct Mammoth-St. Anthony Mine at Tiger, Pinal County, Arizona, was one of the best. There, as if its own color were not sufficiently attractive, sparkling, needle-like, emerald-colored crystals were found sprinkled on pale blue chrysocolla with bright orange wulfenite crystals for accent. ¶ Thicker crystals, up to 2 inches long and a half-inch thick, have been found at Mindouli and elsewhere in the Congo. Some of the specimens, a few inches across and lined with emerald-like jewels of dioptase crystals, have been preserved as small pockets. Some specimens, especially those from Guchab, Otavi, Tsumeb, and elsewhere in South-West Africa, are every bit as good as those from the Congo but are associated with other species, such as calcite, descloizite, and cerussite. If these are coating the dioptase, there is a considerable problem in dissolving them without destroying the entire specimen. Fortunately for the collector, many of the specimens have large, fine crystals with no coatings at all.

HARDNESS	5
SPECIFIC GRAVITY	3.3
COLOR	emerald-green
CRYSTALS	hexagonal: bright, well formed, sometimes short and stubby or long and needle-like

1.

2.

3.

4.

5.

6.

Pages 74-75: Dioptase from Mammoth Mine, Tiger, Pinal County, Arizona. 1. Up to ¾-inch emerald-green crystals from Guchab, South-West Africa; 2. A transparent, green crystal-spray from Mammoth Mine—often such crystals occur with orange wulfenite; 3. A ball of crystals radiating from one center from Mammoth Mine; 4. Bright small crystals partially coated with descloizite and calcite from South-West Africa; 5. A cavity into which ½-inch crystals have grown, from Mindouli, Congo. 6. Large, 1-inch emerald-green crystal on calcite, from Tsumeb, South-West Africa.

Calcite

Calcite

Calcite, which is calcium carbonate, occurs in almost as overwhelming a variety of shapes and colors as quartz. It is also, as is quartz, a very common species, occurring widely in all sorts of deposits, except in granites and rocks of similar origin. Despite its variety, calcite is one of the easiest minerals to identify. A good test is to put a drop of acid, or even vinegar, on powdered calcite, which will cause it to effervesce, or bubble vigorously. If the calcite is well-crystallized, as it usually is, its cleavage will identify it, because it cleaves readily into rhombs. Calcite, like its cousin limestone, is readily attacked by rainwater containing dissolved carbon dioxide, a weak acid that rapidly dissolves calcium carbonate and then carries it to sea, where it is deposited as limestone. In the course of the continuous dissolving and redissolving of this chemically vulnerable species, there is ample opportunity for crystals to form from solutions. ¶ Crystals range from microscopic size to several feet across. Well-formed individual crystals weighing several hundred pounds have been found. Crystal color is variable. Although most specimens are colorless, they can be brown, yellow, violet-green, or pink. Often, when the crystal-growing solutions are full of foreign material, the growth of calcite crystals is not impeded but rather enhanced by the impurities that are swept up in quantity and entombed as inclusions. There are occurrences of such calcite crystals in South Dakota and France, where crystals, although shaped as one would expect, are in large part made of sand. They are commonly called sand calcites. ¶ In the United States, superb crystals and crystal groups have been found in great abundance at the lead-zinc mines of the tri-state district of Kansas, Missouri, and Oklahoma. Violet, amber, yellow, and colorless crystals occur there in many forms, sometimes of enormous size and usually aesthetically associated with galena and sphalerite, among other species. Many of the finest calcite specimens have come from English mines, particularly in Cumberland. Most significant specimens are from Frizington, Egremont, and Alston Moor. The Stank Mine in Lancashire is one of the best-known mines among collectors because of its spectacular groups of pointed, gem-like, transparent crystals.

HARDNESS	3
SPECIFIC GRAVITY	2.7
COLOR	brown, yellow, green, violet, pink, colorless
CRYSTALS	hexagonal: several twin laws are known; sometimes large; scalenohedrons common; many combinations of forms

1.

Pages 78-79: Calcite from Santa Eulalia, Chihuahua, Mexico. 1. Colorless, 2-inch, prismatic crystals from Egremont, Cumberland, England; 2. Translucent, 3-inch, twinned crystals from Egremont; 3. Pea-like calcite from near Carlsbad, Bohemia, Czechoslovakia; 4. Multiple crystals from Mahoning Mine, near Cave-in-Rock, Hardin County, Illinois; 5. Calcite crystals outlined by pyrite crystals from Potosí Mine, San Luis Potosí, Mexico; 6. Disordered stacks of thin white crystals from Andreasberg, Harz Mountains, West Germany.

3.

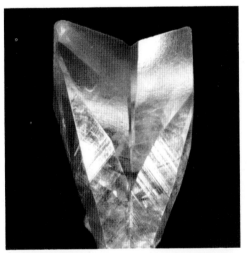

2.

4.

5.

6.

Mimetite

Mimetite

Mimetite is the arsenic-rich member of the lead chlor arsenate-phosphate series of minerals. It is not as common as pyromorphite, the phosphate-rich member, nor does it usually occur as well-crystallized. However, the mineral kingdom is full of surprises. Some large, gem-like, transparent, pale yellow crystals of mimetite have been found in recent times at Tsumeb, South-West Africa, that are better than any known crystals of pyromorphite or mimetite. Specimens of mimetite are usually thick crusts or globules—bright yellow, yellow-orange, orange, or brown—on rock, the best of which come from Mexico. Interesting form and spectacular color easily compensate for any lack of distinct crystals. ¶ Attractive crystallized specimens are known from several places. Except for color, they often look like hexagonal-shaped barrel crystals of pyromorphite. Even the name "mimetite" refers to the way this mineral mimics pyromorphite. A frequent tendency of mimetite toward a yellowish or orange color further blurs the distinction. There are perfect half-inch, yellow-green, hexagonal crystals of mimetite from Johanngeorgenstadt, Saxony, East Germany, that could easily be mistaken for pyromorphite. As does pyromorphite, mimetite tends to form crystals with curved faces—sometimes to the extreme. Campylite, a variety from Dry Gill, Caldbeck Fells, Cumberland, England, has such curved faces that the crystals look almost like yellow to red to brown spheres. ¶ This species, like pyromorphite, is found as a secondary mineral produced from the oxidation and alteration of lead or lead-zinc ores. As expected, it occurs with other species that can be derived from the same ores. This may include cerussite, a lead carbonate; smithsonite, a zinc carbonate; anglesite, a lead sulfate; hemimorphite, a zinc silicate; vanadinite, a lead vanadate; or wulfenite, a lead molybdate.

HARDNESS	3.5 to 4
SPECIFIC GRAVITY	7.2
COLOR	yellow-green, yellow, yellow-orange, orange, brown
CRYSTALS	hexagonal: long barrels, sometimes with curved faces; tapering needles, sometimes transparent

1.

1.

Pages 82-83: Mimetite from San Pedro Corralitos, San Luis Potosí, Mexico. 1. A coating of transparent, needle-like, ⅜-inch crystals from Tsumeb, South-West Africa; 2. Scattered clusters of opaque crystals of the same size from Tsumeb; 3. Large crystal, an inch long and ¾-inch thick, coated with green bayldonite, from Tsumeb; 4. Orange crystals of the prized variety campylite, with rounded faces and curved edges, from Dry Gill, Caldbeck Fells, Cumberland, England; 5. Transparent, ¾-inch, flawless crystals from Tsumeb.

2.

4.

3.

5.

Pyromorphite

Many a mineral collector's most highly prized species come from ore veins that have been oxidized and altered over long periods of time. Pyromorphite is another example of the attractive species originating in such an environment. Because it is a lead chlor phosphate it will aways be derived from lead or lead-zinc ores that also have an available source of phosphorus. If phosphorus is absent but arsenic is present, then mimetite, the lead chlor arsenate, is more likely to form. We find in nature that both phosphorus and arsenic are often available. This means that any number of minerals can form in a given situation with their composition somewhere between that of pure pyromorphite and pure mimetite. Thus, pyromorphite-mimetite is an excellent example of an isomorphous series. ¶ Pyromorphite is not a common mineral and is never found in large amounts sufficient for mining as an ore of lead. It is more abundant, however, than the related species mimetite. Most secondary lead minerals are quite dense, and pyromorphite is no exception. The clues to its identification are high density, a green to tan to brown color, a greasy to splendent luster, and barrel-like hexagonal crystals. Although perfectly formed crystals are found, most specimens have curved faces, are hollowed-out skeletons, or are grouped in nearly parallel clusters. ¶ There never have been enough good pyromorphite specimens from any occurrence to satisfy the demand for them. Bright-green, well-formed, and lustrous hexagonal crystals from Phoenixville, Pennsylvania, and curved or parallel groups of light tan to gray crystals from Bad Ems, and elsewhere in Germany, are highly prized. Specimens of both kinds are sometimes available. Those from Pennsylvania come from the recycling of old collections—the mines have not been operative for over fifty years—while those from Bad Ems, West Germany, could very well be newly mined. Through the years, quality specimens have come also from such widely scattered places as Beresovsk in Russia, Pribram in Czechoslovakia, Shoshone County in Idaho, and Broken Hill in New South Wales, Australia.

HARDNESS	3.5 to 4
SPECIFIC GRAVITY	7
COLOR	brown, green, tan, yellow, orange
CRYSTALS	hexagonal: 6-sided barrels; small, up to an inch or more; hollow, tapered, curved; often in parallel groups

1.

Pages 86-87: Pyromorphite from Merkur Mine, Bad Ems, Nassau, West Germany. 1. A cluster of pale, yellow-green, ½-inch crystals closely resembling mimetite, from Casbachthal, near Erpel, West Germany; 2. Divergent group of tan-colored, almost parallel crystals from Merkur Mine; 3. Dark green, ¼-inch crystals showing typical hollow centers and curved edges, from Wheatley Mine, Phoenixville, Chester County, Pennsylvania; 4. Ball-like, radiating clusters of slender, almost black crystals from Broken Hill, New South Wales, Australia; 5. Well-formed brown crystals up to 1½ inches long from Broken Hill.

2.

3.

4.

5.

Vanadinite

Vanadinite

Vanadinite is found as a secondary mineral resulting from the oxidation and alteration of lead ores. Because it is a lead vanadate, the element vanadium, which gives the species its name, must be present in the altering ore veins. There are several similarities among vanadinite and two other closely related species, pyromorphite and mimetite. All three occur in very well-formed, not too large, hexagonal-shaped crystals. Sometimes the crystals are only partially developed and have hollow centers. These are called skeletal, or cavernous, crystals and resemble the towers of an English castle. Vanadinite has a unique feature: Crystals from certain occurrences are brilliant red-orange, considerably more red than orange. Of course, they may also be a dull brown and an odd silvery gray but never a pyromorphite green or a mimetite yellow-green. ¶ Of the three, vanadinite has the largest crystals reported. Thick crystals measuring up to 5 inches have come from occurrences near Abenab in South-West Africa. They have bright red-orange cores but, unfortunately, are coated with a thick, rough, brown crust of descloizite. Although not objects of beauty, they are coveted by collectors of unusual specimens. Some of the most spectacular and beautiful specimens have come from Miblaben, Morocco. Tabular, hexagonal crystals, up to an inch or more across, that are bright red to rich brown have been found there scattered over light-colored rock in attractive clusters. These are easily the best available, especially since the supply of good specimens from the southwestern United States has been reduced. The best of the latter were probably from the Apache Mine in Arizona. Crystals from there have never been larger than a half inch but they are brilliant red, bright and sparkling, and scattered thickly over rock. Very handsome, half-inch, rich red-brown crystals scattered on white calcite have come from the San Carlos Mine in northern Mexico. The finest specimens of endlichite have also been found in northern Mexico, especially from the Sierra de Los Lamentos Mine in Chihuahua. Endlichite is an arsenic-bearing variety of vanadinite, and at Sierra de Los Lamentos it is found in jumbles of curved and tapering, brilliant, but very dark brown, crystals.

HARDNESS	2.5 to 3
SPECIFIC GRAVITY	6.5 to 7
COLOR	red-orange, red, red-brown, yellowish brown, dark brown
CRYSTALS	hexagonal: cavernous, curved, tapered; usually 6-sided tabular or elongated

1.

2.

3.

4.

Pages 90-91: Vanadinite from Mibladen, Morocco. 1. A cavernous, multiple, orange-brown crystal, 1½ inches across, from Mibladen; 2. Tapered, needle-like, dark brown endlichite crystals, a variety of vanadinite, from Villa Ahumada, Sierra de Los Lamentos, Chihuahua, Mexico; 3. Hollow, 1½-inch orange-brown hexagonal crystal from San Carlos Mine, Chihuahua, Mexico; 4. A group of bright orange hexagonal plates from Mibladen, where crystal colors vary from brilliant red through orange to dark brown; 5. Orange-tan aggregated groups of semi-parallel crystals from San Carlos Mine.

5.

Prehnite

Prehnite is a mineral species that rarely forms crystals large enough to excite the interest of a mineral collector. In 1972, a few specimens were found in the mines at Asbestos, Quebec, with excellent white crystals measuring a half inch and more in length. Their appeal is due to their rarity, and they have little to offer aesthetically. The charm and appeal of most prehnite lies in its color—a pale to medium green, gray-green, or yellowish green—and in its thick, interesting, sculptural crusts over the other rocks and minerals. Aside from the crystals found in Quebec, perhaps the most coveted are the bright green, curved-crystal aggregates found years ago at Bourg d'Oisans, Dauphiné, France. ¶ Prehnite begins as an outpouring of dark lava from deep within the earth. As pressures are released, water is freed. With any available surface water, it percolates through the lava, dissolving out sodium, potassium, calcium, aluminum, and silica, which are deposited in gas pockets and cracks developed in the cooling, shrinking lava. Prehnite, a calcium aluminum silicate, is often deposited in large quantities with other minerals. Associated with it are apophyllite, pectolite, datolite, and the zeolites, a group of almost thirty closely related minerals. Many of these are well-crystallized and make very attractive specimens. Because all the associated minerals are usually white or colorless, except for greenish datolite, prehnite gives them a colorful background ¶ The most beautiful prehnite specimens come from the Watchung Mountains of northern New Jersey. Rocks there are the remains of ancient lava flows. They are dark gray to black, very dense, and are referred to as trap rock. Such quarries as those at West Paterson, Prospect Park, and Bound Brook have been operated for years for crushed stone used in road building and construction. There are good prehnite-yielding trap rocks elsewhere, such as in the well-known quarry at Centreville, Fairfax County, Virginia, probably more famous for its magnificent apophyllite crystals associated with prehnite. Many other enormous lava flows, like those of Oregon and Washington, yield fine zeolites and other related species but no prehnite.

HARDNESS	6.5
SPECIFIC GRAVITY	2.8 to 3
COLOR	white to green, yellow, yellow-green, gray-green
CRYSTALS	orthorhombic: rare, small; ideal crystals up to a half inch; curved-crystal aggregates of more than an inch

1.

2.

Pages 94-95: Prehnite from West Paterson, Passaic County, New Jersey. 1. Stalactite-like aggregations of crystals from trap rock quarries near Paterson, New Jersey; 2. An almost spherical, 1½-inch aggregate of crystals, with its most distinct crystal development around the equator, from near Centreville, Fairfax County Virginia; 3. Small light-green balls of crystals from Prospect Park Quarry, Passaic County, New Jersey; 4. Simple, large free-standing crystals, up to an inch long, from Asbestos, Quebec; 5. A prehnite cast of an original group of glauberite crystals now dissolved away.

3.

4.

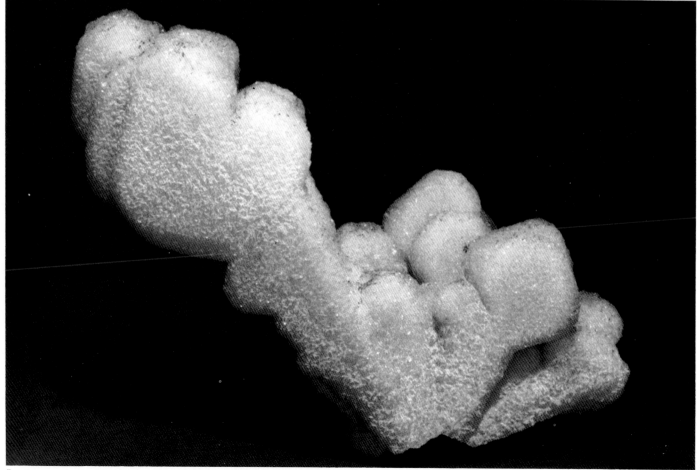

5.

Rutile

Rutile

Rutile crystallizes well and in such a variety of ways that several specimens can be in a collection without any appearance of repetition. Graves Mountain, Georgia, has, over a period of time, furnished large numbers of brilliant, well-formed, single crystals up to several inches across. At Champion Mine, near Laws, California, similar crystals occur except that they tend to be smaller, brighter, and better formed. ¶ One of the more attractive characteristics of rutile is that its crystals tend to form as twins. These may take the form of a cross-hatched network of thick needles lying in the same plane at 120-degree angles looking like some kind of rigid netting. Needle crystals tend to be light red to golden straw-color, whereas the thicker, stubbier crystals of Georgia and California are dark red-brown to black. Often these straw blades, twinned or not, are found as inclusions in clear quartz, called rutilated quartz. Its most spectacular specimens come from Itibiara, Brazil. Rutile and hematite have compatible structures and, in Switzerland and Brazil, hematite crystals occur with thick needles of rutile laid out in fixed directions on the faces of the hematite. ¶ Stubbier, darker-colored rutile crystals also occur as twins. Due to the 120-degree angle the twins often take with each other, and because of their resemblance to knees and elbows, they are called knee twins, elbow twins, or geniculate twins—geniculate meaning knee-like. Other kinds of interesting twinning are also possible with this species. ¶ Rutile is a titanium oxide, and rutile beach sands are mined and processed as an ore of titanium, a metal increasingly in demand because it is very strong and can resist melting even under very high temperatures. Natural rutile, whether dark or light in color, is rarely transparent enough, even in small pieces, for gems. However, it is now possible to manufacture very pure and transparent rutile crystals in several colors or almost without color. Under various trade names, such as Titania, cut gems of rutile are offered at reasonable prices. They are very attractive because of their high dispersion of light but they scratch easily when mounted in jewelry.

HARDNESS	6 to 6.5
SPECIFIC GRAVITY	4.2
COLOR	red-brown to black, needle crystals—light red to straw yellow
CRYSTALS	tetragonal: stubby, well-formed; also in thick needles; frequently twinned

1.

2.

3.

4.

5.

Pages 98-99: *Rutile from near Boiling
Springs, Cleveland County, North Carolina.
1. Rutilated quartz with embedded needles
and blades of golden-yellow rutile from
Itibiara, Bahia, Brazil; 2. A dark, 1-inch
single crystal with muscovite from Stony
Point, Alexander County, North Carolina;
3. Rutilated quartz with embedded
needles oriented around a crystal of hematite
to form a star, from Itibiara; 4. Perfect
butterfly-type twin crystals from Cerrado
Frio, Minas Gerais, Brazil; 5. Typical
twin crystals from Yadkin County, North
Carolina, with each bend at a 114-degree
angle representing additional twinning.*

Marcasite

Marcasite

In poorly crystallized masses marcasite is easily confused with pyrite, its near relative. For many years the name marcasite was used for pyrite, and the confusion was only resolved around the end of the eighteenth century. Both marcasite and pyrite are sulfides of iron with exactly the same chemical composition. The difference between them is in their structure and their crystallography. Marcasite is orthorhombic, and pyrite is isometric. Consequently, they form very different kinds of crystals and behave differently in many other ways. While pyrite can form in nature under almost any conditions, marcasite forms in low-temperature deposits. Thus, it is commonly found both in clays and other sediments and as concretions, stalactites, and encrustations of other substances. ¶ Marcasite is unusually abundant in the low-temperature lead-zinc ore deposits of the Mississippi Valley, where it occurs beautifully crystallized, sometimes covering rocks several feet across. The crystals are usually repeatedly twinned to produce fan-like groups called cockscombs—which they much resemble. Often these bright metallic sprays are associated with fine crystals of galena, sphalerite, chalcopyrite, calcite, and dolomite. ¶ Although marcasite has a metallic luster, it is seldom splendent like its cousin, pyrite. Marcasite's color, too, is a somewhat pale brassy yellow that tends to tarnish rather quickly, taking on a dull gray-green color—more gray than green. For some reason, certain marcasite specimens are chemically unstable and, after sitting years or even days in a collection, will gradually become dusted with a white coating of iron sulfate. Some specimens may even decompose to the point where they fall apart to a heap of gravel. Generally, however, specimens that have been washed and very carefully dried remain quite stable. Some of the spearhead marcasite crystals that were dug from the chalk cliffs of Dover, England, almost a century ago are still in excellent condition in collections.

HARDNESS	6 to 6.5
SPECIFIC GRAVITY	4.9
COLOR	pale brass-yellow, tarnishing to dull gray-green
CRYSTALS	orthorhombic: twinned cockscombs, odd-shaped concretions

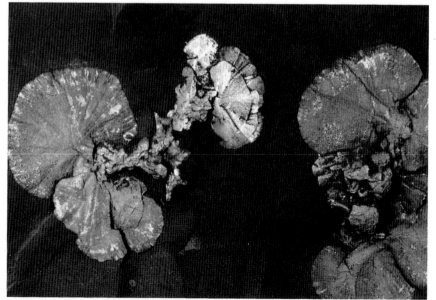

1.

2.

3.

Pages 102-103: *Marcasite from Herne, Westphalia, West Germany. 1. Bright metallic, flat concretions in gray shale— not fossils although resembling plant life— from Germany; 2. Twinned crystal groups of cockscomb marcasite from Picher, Ottawa County, Oklahoma; 3. Flat, 2½-inch, sunburst concretions known as marcasite but probably pyrite, its near relative, from Hardin County, Illinois; 4. A fat, worm-like concretion of pyrite, or a mixture of pyrite and marcasite, from near Folkstone, Kent, England; 5. Odd, hollow stalactites of marcasite from New Diggings, Lafayette County, Wisconsin.*

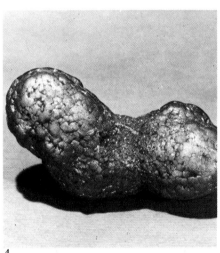

4.

5.

Pyrite

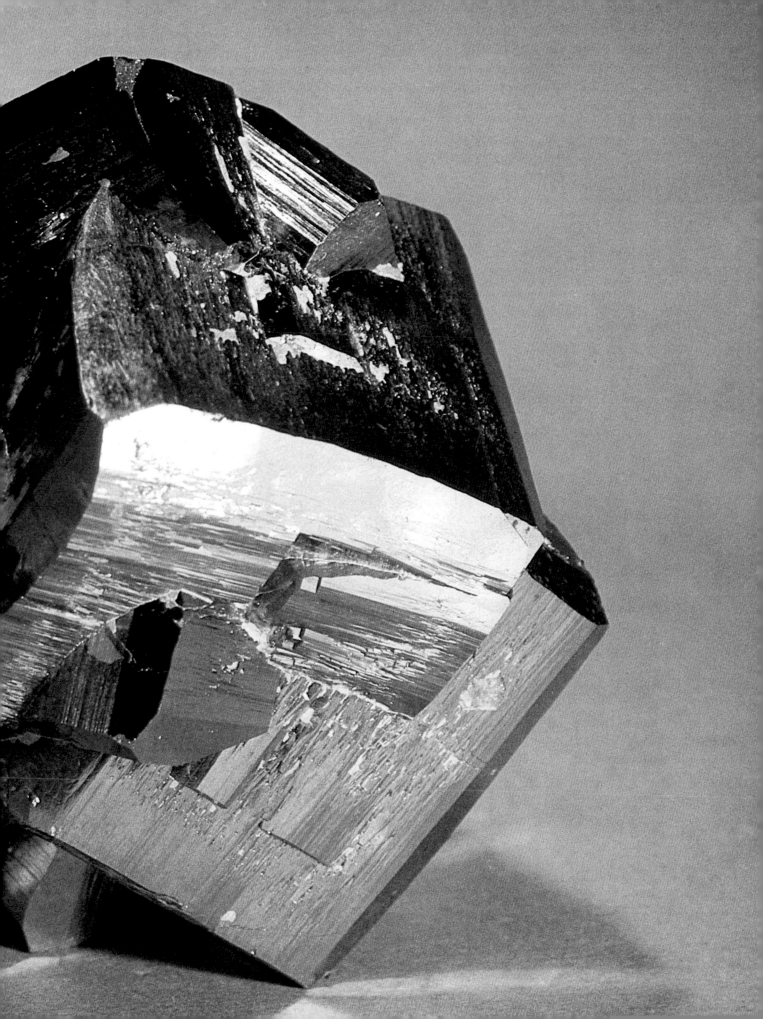

Pyrite

Pyrite Japan, Spain, Italy, and Norway mine the bulk of pyrite, which, being a compound of iron and sulfur, supplies about forty percent of the world's sulfur. Although these countries are the major producers, pyrite occurs in just about every country in the world. It also occurs in various types of deposits, from those formed in sediments of near-freezing temperatures to those formed from molten rock. Pyrite is the most common mineral in ore veins. There are thick beds of pyrite in Spain that are as much as a mile long. ¶ Because it is so widespread and in such quantity, it seems reasonable that fine specimens would be fairly common. They are. This species crystallizes well, and the shiny, brassy crystals, in sizes up to a foot across, that are found in most collections come from several places. Pyrite specimens keep quite well in collections because the mineral is hard enough to withstand minor abuse and chemically stable enough, unless it is associated with marcasite or some other relatively unstable species, to stay bright and shiny. ¶ Even with numerous excellent occurrences there are a few that stand out as producers of the most desirable specimens. The iron mines at Rio Marina on the island of Elba have long supplied superb pyrite crystals, usually associated with sparkling, black hematite flakes. These crystals come in almost every conceivable form of the species, with perhaps the best being the splendent big pyritohedrons with mirror-like faces. ¶ Large shiny octahedrons are the special trademark of certain pyrite crystals from Bolivia and Peru. Specimens from Pennsylvania, Utah, and Colorado have their particular differences by which they can be recognized. Flattened, 3- to 5-inch, sun-like disks of pyrite can only have come from the coal shales of Illinois. As with galena, calcite, quartz, and a few other species, a collector could easily specialize in building a fine collection of pyrite alone.

HARDNESS	6 to 6.5
SPECIFIC GRAVITY	5.02
COLOR	brass-yellow
CRYSTALS	isometric: bright pyritohedrons, cubes, or a combination of the two; replaces other materials to form pseudomorphs

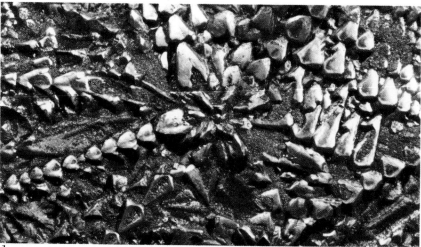

1.

2.

3.

4.

Pages 106-107: Pyrite from Llogrono, Ambasaguas, Spain. 1. Radiating spears of pyrite dendrites in clay, from near Fort Scott, Bourbon County, Kansas; 2. Cube with typical surface striations, a common pyrite form, from Brosso, Piedmont, Italy; 3. Fossil mollusk competely replaced by pyrite; 4. A 2-inch ball of crystals, which started growth at the center and whose surface is a mosaic of crystal faces; 5. Pyrite replacement of a shell from near Farmington, Knox County, Illinois; 6. An overgrowth of pyrite on the face of a cube, called cathedral pyrite in reference to the arched shapes.

5.

6.

Proustite

Proustite is one of the two important ruby-silver species. The common name refers to the fact that proustite and pyrargyrite, its near relative, are both silver-bearing minerals that show a strong red color when held up to light. Proustite and pyrargyrite are often confused with each other because they have similar crystals, color, and luster. It is even possible that both may occur in the same silver deposit. There are, of course, tests that can be used to distinguish between proustite, a silver arsenic sulfide, and pyrargyrite, a silver antimony sulfide. The fact remains, however, that until collectors acquire considerable experience with the two they can be easily confused. ¶ Because proustite is a silver mineral and is colorful, often well-crystallized, and relatively rare, it is an ideal species for a collector. Unfortunately, the supply of good, undamaged specimens has always been so limited (there are not enough to satisfy even a small part of the demand) that prices tend to be among the highest of the ore minerals—approaching those of the gem minerals. Without question, the finest specimens were recovered, many years ago, from the Dolores Mine at Chanarcillo, Chile. At this mine, an occasional crystal reached 3 inches in length, and many were almost transparent. Unfortunately, proustite is soft and is cursed with the characteristic of blackening on exposure to bright light or to any light for long periods of time. This combination of defects has destroyed or greatly reduced the appeal and value of a large proportion of the crystals recovered. Those still in their pristine state have become rare as Rembrandts, although not yet as expensive. ¶ Very good specimens have come also from several mines in East Germany, especially in Saxony, and from Jachymov, in Bohemia, Czechoslovakia. The same disadvantages hold for these specimens. In spite of years of production, the total of unspoiled proustite specimens from any occurrence is small.

HARDNESS	2 to 2.5
SPECIFIC GRAVITY	5.6
COLOR	red, changes to black on exposure to excess light
CRYSTALS	hexagonal: tapered crystals of triangular cross section, sometimes columnar crystals with hexagonal cross section

Three of these proustite crystals,
and that on pages 110-111, are from the
Dolores Mine, Chanarcillo, Chile; they
are excellent specimens but are antiques
recovered about a century ago.
1. A 3-inch single crystal with interesting
growth figures on its faces; 2. Crystals
with strong vertical striations, which
are typical of the species;
3. A crystal with multiple twinning;
4. A fine, ruby-colored twin
crystal, found a few years ago, from
Neiderschlema, East Germany,
the only recent source of
large proustite crystals.

2.

1.

3.

4.

Galena

Galena

Galena occurs in such a variety of specimens from so many different mines that it is possible to make a specialty collection of it alone. If the several species with which it is commonly associated were included, the selection could be broadened greatly. Galena, which chemically is lead sulfide, is the most common ore of lead—its name comes from the Greek word meaning lead ore—and it occurs with other important sulfides, such as sphalerite, chalcopyrite, and pyrite. The extraction of lead from galena is so easy that the method was discovered in earliest times. Fire will melt it, and coals will reduce it to metallic lead. Remelting and skimming off any debris from the top will leave a fairly pure mass of lead. Early settlers in the colonies were able to prepare suitable lead for bullets this way. ¶ In the enormous galena deposits of the tri-state mining district, comprising the adjacent corners of Kansas, Missouri, and Oklahoma, the mineral occurs with splendid amber to lavender crystals of calcite, small saddle-shaped crystals of pink or white dolomite, black to ruby-red crystals of sphalerite, and cockscombs of sharply crystallized marcasite. In these deposits, shiny cubes of galena have been found measuring over 6 inches across, and calcite crystals have been found up to 2 feet long. Aside from crystals of enormous size, the district also produces superior quality specimens of all associated species in manageable sizes for collectors and in large quantities. ¶ A different sort of occurrence at the lead mining districts at Alston Moor and Weardale in England has produced excellent specimens of brilliant and more complex galena crystals associated with some of the finest fluorite specimens known. ¶ The shining, silvery metallic luster and the usually excellent development of galena crystals have contributed to their popularity with collectors. The mineral is rather soft, somewhat easily damaged and has a distressing tendency to cleave along brilliant cube faces. Nevertheless, specimens that have miraculously survived mining operations without being destroyed are durable enough to withstand normal, but careful, handling without being damaged.

HARDNESS	2.5
SPECIFIC GRAVITY	7.6
COLOR	silver-gray to dark metallic gray
CRYSTALS	isometric: cubes, sometimes small octahedrons, or with more complex modifications

1.

3.

2.

Pages 114-115: Galena from Galena, Cherokee County, Kansas. 1. Two-inch cubes from near Peacock City, Cherokee County, Kansas; 2. A 4-inch multiple-crystal cube with its faces obscured by the uneven growth of octahedron faces, from near Treece, Cherokee County, Kansas; 3. Four galena cubes in parallel growth covered by small, oriented galena crystals; 4. Pseudomorphs of hexagonal pyromorphite replaced by galena from near Bernkastel, West Germany; 5. Curved and elongated cubes from Baxter Springs, Kansas.

4.

5.

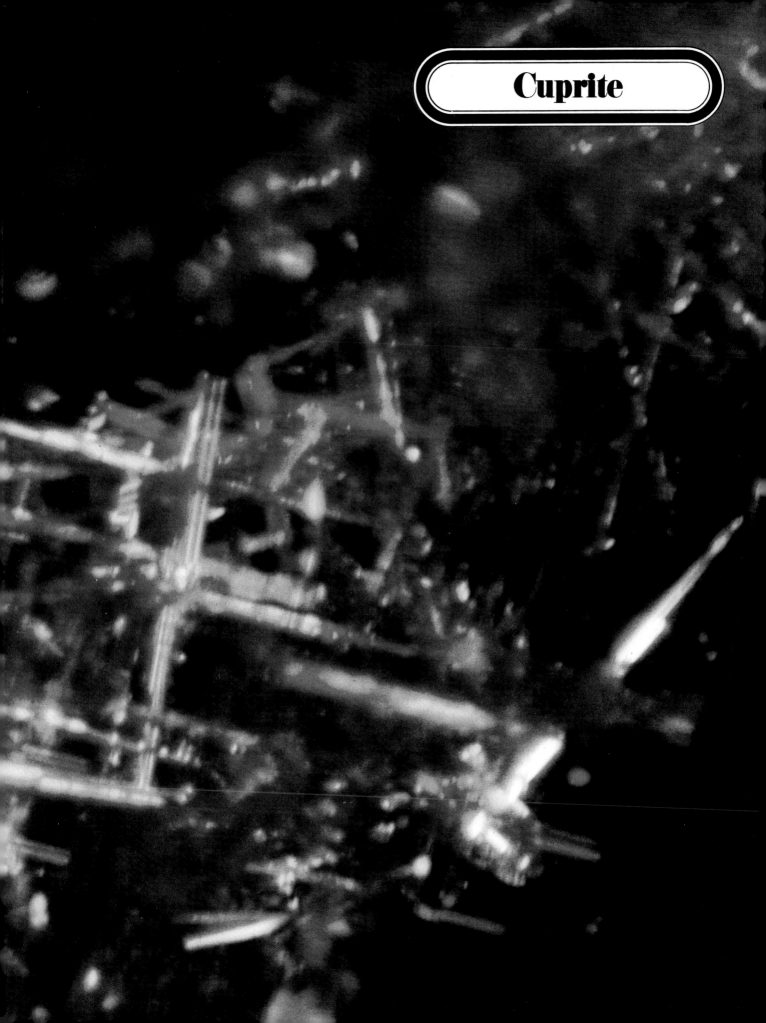

Cuprite

Cuprite

Cuprite is an appropriate name for this species. It comes from the Latin word *cuprum,* meaning copper. Cuprite is not only a copper mineral—copper oxide—but it is usually found associated with native copper, from which it commonly forms. The most striking feature of this species is its bright and strong orange-red to purple-red color. It crystallizes well, with the crystals tending to be small, highly modified cubes or octahedrons. Crystals a quarter inch or more across are unusual. Larger crystals tend to be a darker purplish red and they gradually blacken when exposed to strong light or atmospheric pollutants. ¶ Often, cuprite crystals tend to form as tangled masses of orange-red fibers, each of which is actually a grossly elongated single crystal. This form is called chalcotrichite, which means copper hairs. Although extremely attractive, such masses are difficult to preserve because they are so delicate. The masses of fibers are easily squashed and matted, even with careful handling, and are impossible to wash if they get dusty. However, these specimens are attractive enough to deserve the special care they need. Sometimes chalcotrichite hairs are included in other crystals, such as calcite or mimetite, as they form. Their color turns the host crystals bright orange-red. ¶ The cuprite occurrence at Chessy, near Lyon, France, has furnished numerous well-formed large crystals of cuprite that have been altered on the surface to bright green malachite—another copper mineral. Occasionally, the surface alteration may even be to bright blue azurite—still another copper species. Perhaps the best occurrences for chalcotrichite have been the copper mines of Tsumeb, South-West Africa, of Cornwall, England, and of Bisbee, Arizona. These and other mines have also furnished collectors with the more normal deep-red crystal groups.

HARDNESS	3.5 to 4
SPECIFIC GRAVITY	6.14
COLOR	orange-red to purple-red
CRYSTALS	isometric: smooth-faced cubes, octahedrons modified by other forms, crystal hairs

1.

2.

3.

Pages 118-119: Chalcotrichite—seen here under microscope—from Redruth, Cornwall, England. 1. Once a mass of interlocking copper wires, now its partially altered surface is coated with tiny, red cuprite crystals, from Copper Queen Mine, Bisbee, Cochise County, Arizona; 2. A stack of ¼-inch, shiny, well-formed, deep-red cubes from near Liskeard, Cornwall, England; 3. Half-inch dodecahedron (l.) and skeletal octahedron crystals with cuprite cores altered on the surface to bright green malachite, from Chessy, near Lyon, France; 4. A jumble of ¼-inch dark-red crystals of cuprite, and copper from which it formed, from Bisbee.

4.

Erythrite

Erythrite

Erythrite and annabergite, its blood relative, are species of no particular importance to anyone but mineral collectors. Both species are arsenates of cobalt and nickel. Actually, there is a complete series of minerals with chemical compositions between the two, ranging in color all the way from purplish red erythrite, at the cobalt-rich end of the series, to yellow-green annabergite, at the nickel-rich end of the series. Both species are found as secondary minerals at, or near, surfaces where exposures of other cobalt and nickel arsenides and sulfides, such as cobaltite, niccolite, or smaltite, have been weathered and altered. The brilliant magenta and green coatings and crusts are telltale indications of the presence of cobalt and nickel deposits. ¶ Crystals of these two species are quite rare and are usually microscopic in size. These species, when found in any quantity at all, are likely to be only earthy crusts. Sizable crystals are difficult to preserve. So soft that a fingernail can scratch them, the crystals are also distressingly flexible and are bent over by the least pressure. Even worse, they exhibit a strong tendency to cleave in very thin plates along the flat, bladed direction of the crystals. All in all, they are among the most difficult crystallized specimens to find and to keep undamaged once they are acquired. This, of course, makes them all the more challenging to a collector. ¶ The best specimens of erythrite seen in collections have undoubtedly come from any of three noted occurrences. Those recovered from the Sara Alicia Mine near Alamos, Sonora, Mexico, have coatings of tiny needle-like magenta-colored crystals that make the specimens look as if they were covered in pinkish purple velvet. Those from the mines of Schneeberg, Saxony, East Germany, are longer and larger needle-like crystals that look like sprays of very elongated and narrow purple blades. From near Bou Azzer in Morocco come the best crystals of all, many of which are assemblages of bold, broad purplish blades up to an inch long and a half inch wide with variable thicknesses. ¶ Strangely, good specimens of annabergite do not exist except as a variety with considerable magnesium in its composition. This variety is called cabrerite and comes from ancient silver mines at Laurium, Greece. In everything except their green color, these crystals, up to a quarter inch long, look and behave like erythrite.

	HARDNESS	SPECIFIC GRAVITY	COLOR	CRYSTALS
Erythrite	1.5 to 2.5	3	magenta	monoclinic: thin elongate blades
Annabergite	2.5 to 3	3	apple-green	monoclinic: thin elongate blades

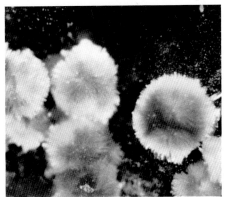

1.

2.

3.

4.

Pages 122-123: Erythrite—seen here under microscope—from Sara Alicia Mine, near Alamos, Sonora, Mexico. 1. Tiny balls of velvety erythrite—seen under microscope as clusters of tiny needle-like crystals—from Sara Alicia Mine; 2. Remarkable, ¾-inch crystals lining a rock cavity from Bou Azzer, Morocco; 3. A spray of 1½-inch needles from the old Rappold Mine, Schneeberg, Saxony, East Germany, which, along with others in the area, furnished for years the finest specimens; 4. Crystals over an inch long from a newer find near Bou Azzer.

Garnet

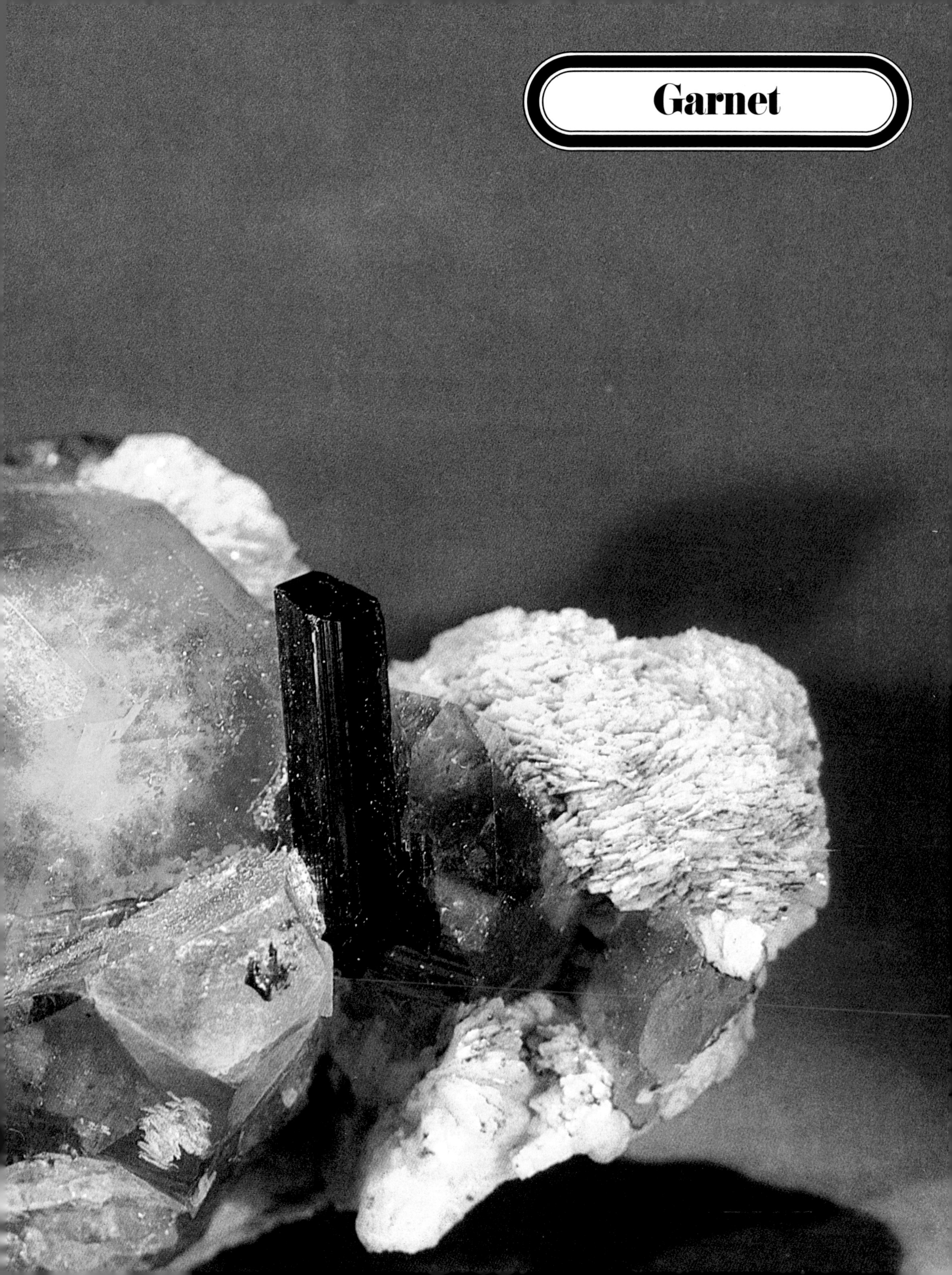

Garnet

Antique jewelry set with Bohemian garnets has come back into fashion, from having gone into a decline after the Victorian era. Because of its old-time and renewed popularity, the idea has developed that garnet is always red-brown or dark, purplish red. Some of it is, but much of it is not. Except for blue, every color is represented by some kind of garnet. The other misconception, even among collectors, is that garnet is the name of a single mineral species. It is really the name of a family of six or so species. Mineralogists recognize six major kinds of garnet and admit, at the same time, that rarely does any of the six occur in pure form. Some of their compositions are so grossly intermixed that it is difficult to determine what the mix is. The six species fall into two groups. One group includes uvarovite (the calcium-chromium garnet), grossular (the calcium-aluminum garnet), and andradite (the calcium-iron garnet). The other group includes pyrope (the magnesium-aluminum garnet), almandine (the iron-aluminum garnet), and spessartine (the manganese-aluminum garnet). There is some, but not much, mingling between the two groups and a rather free mixing within each. ¶ Garnets are popular collection species. Invariably, they are well-crystallized in 12-sided dodecahedrons or 24-sided trapezohedrons—or some combination of the two. It is actually difficult to find garnets that are not well-formed. Sometimes the crystals are too big to handle. In the commercial almandine deposit at Gore Mountain, New York, crystals a foot across are common, and they have been known to reach 3 feet. At Dalsfjord, Norway, there are crystals weighing over an estimated 500 pounds each. Of course, collectors prefer perfect crystals 6 inches in diameter or less. ¶ Because of their strong crystallizing ability and variable composition, garnets are able to form in all sorts of rocks in a wide range of temperatures and pressures. This makes it a very widespread group of species. Because garnets are highly resistant to weathering they persist after their host rocks have decomposed. This accounts for enormous deposits of garnet sands big enough to be mined.

GARNET	HARDNESS	SPECIFIC GRAVITY	COLOR	CRYSTALS (ALL SPECIES)
Pyrope	7	3.5	orange-red, deep red, purple-red	isometric: dodecahedrons and trapezohedrons
Almandine	7	4.3	dark red, brownish red, purplish red	
Spessartine	7	4.2	orange-red, orange, yellow-orange	
Uvarovite	7.5	3.5	green	
Grossular	6.5	3.5	white, colorless, yellowish, grayish, pale green, orange-red, yellowish orange, reddish brown, pink	
Andradite	7	3.8	brown to black, olive, brownish green, emerald-green, yellow, brownish red	

1.

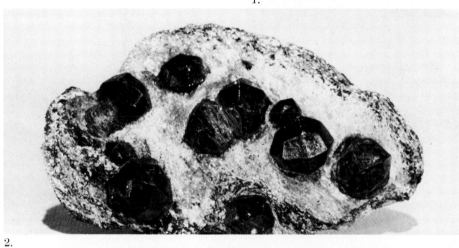

2.

Pages 126-127: *Spessartine with schorl from Hercules Mine, Ramona, San Diego County, California. 1. Two-inch almandine trapezohedrons from near Westfield, Massachusetts; 2. Almandine crystals in schist from Fairfield, Connecticut; 3. A single, 5-inch dodechahedron of chlorite-coated almandine from Sedalia Mine, near Salida, Colorado; 4. A 1-inch andradite dodechahedron from Chernyshevsk, Russia; 5. A flattened garnet crystal embedded in mica, a simultaneous growth of almandine and muscovite, from Deer Park Mine, Penland, North Carolina.*

4.

3.

5.

Radioactives

Radioactives

This is one of a group of mineral species that gives off a fascinating kind of emanation called radioactivity. Radioactivity is a spontaneous emission of energy and atomic debris liberated as unstable uranium atoms explode, disintegrate, and eject their parts. The process of disintegration of uranium atoms continues unpredictably and continuously over enormous periods of time. ¶ Uranium minerals can be conveniently separated into two groups, i.e. primary and secondary. The most important primary species is uraninite, which in its massive form was formerly called pitchblende. It is uranium oxide and it is a heavy black mineral originating from hot solutions that come from molten material in the earth's crust. As expected, it is usually found in nature with quartz, feldspar, and mica in coarse granites—pegmatites —that have this kind of origin. ¶ Once uraninite and other primary uranium minerals, such as euxenite, samarskite, and betafite, are deposited, they become subject to chemical attack and weathering. The secondary uranium minerals result from this process. There are numerous secondary uranium species, but torbernite and autunite are the best-known among collectors. They are similar species. Torbernite is a copper uranium phosphate, and autunite a calcium uranium phosphate. Because of the copper in torbernite it is a green mineral, but autunite is yellowish or yellow-green. Because their structures are similar, both species occur in crystals which are thin translucent square plates resembling shiny mica, to which they are not related in any way. ¶ Many of the most spectacular secondary uranium minerals known come from the Shinkolobwe Mine in Katanga, in the south of the Congo. In the United States, more than two thousand different deposits of uranium ore were being worked on the Colorado plateau after World War II in an effort to produce ores for atomic energy. In some places the secondary uranium mineral concentrations were enormous, sometimes spreading over hundreds of feet. Even so, although the ores were rich and many new uranium species appeared, there were very few spectacular specimens for collectors. Such specimens have usually come from rather small and widely scattered deposits.

	HARDNESS	SPECIFIC GRAVITY	COLOR	CRYSTALS
Autunite	2 to 2.5	3.2	yellow, yellow-green	tetragonal: thin square plates; opaque
Torbernite	2 to 2.5	3.2	green	tetragonal: thin square plates; translucent, transparent
Uraninite	5 to 6	7 to 10	black	isometric: crude cubes

1.

2.

3.

4.

5.

Pages 130-131: *Autunite from Daybreak Mine, Mt. Spokane, Spokane County, Washington. 1. Brilliant yellow autunite crystals (calcium uranium phosphate) on rock from Margnac, Haute Vienne, France; 2. Thin, translucent, bright-green torbernite squares from Musonoi, Congo; 3. Black dendritic uraninite crystals (uranium oxide) in feldspar, from Ruggles Mine, Grafton County, New Hampshire; 4. Fat, green, ¼-inch torbernite crystals (copper uranium phosphate) from Aveyron, France; 5. Square, ¼-inch, yellow autunite crystals on feldspar from Daybreak Mine.*

Faceted Gems

Gems are minerals and are therefore often associated with mineral collections. Nature sometimes endows gem minerals with brilliant, flat, crystal faces. Rarely are these faces perfectly smooth or perfectly flat. Rarely are they in the right places to give the gemstone full opportunity to show itself to best advantage. And seldom are the crystal shapes those a craftsman needs to create jewelry. Gem cutting and faceting techniques were developed through the centuries to solve such problems. Interestingly enough, new solutions in technique, machinery, and style are still being developed for the same purpose—to enhance a gemstone's general beauty and utility. ¶ The earliest mention of faceted gems was about A.D. 800, but it was not until the 1600's that serious attention was given to systematic faceting. Now all of the finest pieces of rough gem minerals are routinely converted into faceted stones by cutters known as lapidaries. ¶ The process for faceting a gemstone can be broken down into three steps. First, the stone is sawed roughly to shape. The saw used has no teeth but is a thin, rapidly rotating, circular disk with diamonds embedded in its circumference. Diamonds, being extremely hard, actually scratch through the gem. Once sawed roughly to shape, the faces—or facets—are ground against a "lap," a horizontally placed rotating disk, with the appropriate grinding abrasive applied to the surface. The position of the gem is precisely controlled by a faceting head, mounted over the lap. This device holds the stone and makes it possible to set the stone against the lap at a predetermined angle so that each facet is ground in precisely the right place. Once properly faceted, the lapping process is repeated with a much finer abrasive to give the gem its final, brilliant polish. ¶ Through the years, many different "cuts," or sets of facets, have been designed for different gem species and for different purposes. There are cuts called baguettes, triangles, kites, keystones, marquises, and many others. To describe the various cuts, a stone is figuratively divided into three sections. The flat top is called the table. Facets around the table and above the middle of the gem are called crown facets. The middle is called the girdle, and facets below the girdle are called pavilion facets. The placement of facets should be different for each species because the light reflection and refraction characteristics of each are different. However, this aspect of faceting is usually ignored because popular taste almost always insists on two standard cuts—the step cut and the standard brilliant cut. The step cut is the kind usually used for aquamarine, emerald, tourmaline, and other colored gems. The standard brilliant cut is universally used for diamond.

1.

Pages 134-135: Gem crystals and faceted gems, including a 12,000-carat topaz sphere. The gems illustrated in photographs 1, 3, 4, 5, and 6 are examples of different cutting styles used for faceted gems. The brilliant cut, illustrated in number 5, and the modified step, or emerald, cut, illustrated in numbers 3 and 4, are commonly used for commercial gems. More unusual cuts, such as those in photographs 1 and 6, are frequently used for special purposes. Highly-colored gems often have flat tops to best display their color. The gems in photograph 2 illustrate a sequence in the production of a standard brilliant cut.

3.

2.

4.

5.

6.

Gem Carvings

Gem Carvings

Any amateur gemstone cutter in the United States, before 1930, would have found it almost impossible to locate suitable abrasives, machinery, and information. Yet lapidaries in other parts of the world had been successfully cutting gem material for more than 5,000 years. By 1940 conditions changed drastically in the U.S., and today tens of thousands of amateurs are engaged in lapidary work. Contrary to popular belief, the labor of lapidaries throughout time has been expended less on items of jewelry and personal adornment than on *objets d'art*: ashtrays, bookends, Buddhas, elephants, goldfish, Chinese immortals—many of them ordinary. ¶ Currently many objects of high aesthetic and artistic value are being cut worldwide. In the Orient the ancient trade of the skilled gem carvers has been handed down successfully over thousands of years, despite political turmoil. Some jade carvings recently cut in the People's Republic of China are as well-conceived and carved as the best older pieces. The scarcity of quality carving material, rather than a shortage of skill, is the major factor limiting quality production. ¶ Thousands of miles away in Idar-Oberstein, West Germany, gem carvers have also been producing their wares for centuries. Formerly, they were carvers to the Romans. Today, they create the major industry of the twin cities. The tradition is old but the techniques are new. Diamond abrasives and special diamond tools, as well as the best power machinery available, enable German cutters to do superb work. ¶ Unlike faceted stones, carvings are limited in size only by the available material and the weight that can be lifted by hand or by mechanical hoists. The complexity of carvings can vary greatly. Simple surface inscriptions or raised designs on flat pieces require some craftsmanship. Cameos or gem portraits are more difficult because the finished subjects must be recognizable. Three-dimensional gemstone sculptures are most difficult of all. ¶ Modern technology permits gemstone carvings to be made now in a fraction of the time it took earlier lapidaries and with greater ease and less expense. Today, the work of a carver can be a delight to many, rather than a pleasure restricted to the wealthy few.

1.

2.

3.

4.

Pages 138-139: Carved gem objects, including agate dolphins, coral beads, a quartz sphere, and a 10-inch lavender jade figure. 1. A modern agate cameo, measuring 6 inches across, skillfully carved in a traditional style, making use of naturally colored layers, cut in Idar-Oberstein, West Germany; 2. A pair of foot-tall figures in ivory, an easily-worked material, recording Chinese costume as perceived by the artist; ivory is traditionally a gem material although not a mineral; 3. A 3-inch bowl of black jade with delicately thin handles and the very high polish possible only with jade, from Wyoming; 4. A translucent bowl, 7 inches across the rim, cut in Idar-Oberstein.

Rocks

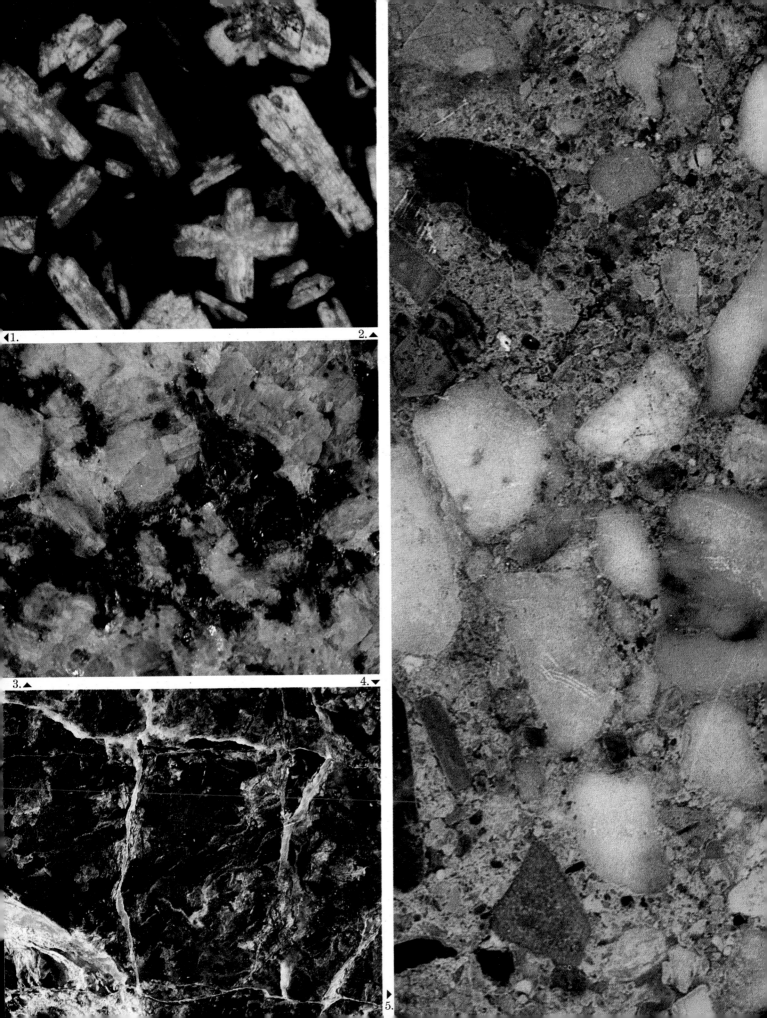

Pages 142-143: 1. Peridotite seen under
a petrographic microscope; 2. Porphyry;
3. Granite; 4. Serpentinite; 5. Breccia.
This page: 1. Schist (metamorphic rock)
showing contorted folds; 2. Oddly formed
clay concretions (sedimentary rock) from
Connecticut; 3. Dark- and light-streaked
marble (metamorphic rock) from Rockland,
Maine; 4. A block of unsplit slate
(metamorphic rock) from West Castleton,
Vermont; 5. Dacite porphyry (igneous rock)
from Shasta County, California; 6. Coquina
(sedimentary rock), or naturally cemented
shells, from Virginia; 7. Conglomerate
(sedimentary rock) of naturally cemented
pebbles, from Devonshire, England.

Rocks There are few people, other than scientists, who collect rocks. Even the popular term "rockhound," which is applied to amateur mineral collectors, is inappropriate. A petrographer, a student of rock types, is well aware that rocks fail to meet the strict definition of minerals. Most rocks, being aggregates of two or more minerals in variable amounts, do not have the relatively fixed composition of mineral species. Granite, for example, is composed of a mixture of grains of quartz and feldspar with some mica added. Sometimes a rock may consist of a single mineral, such as serpentine, but may cover such an enormous territory that it is responsible for a major feature of the earth's surface. Then it is both a rock and a mineral. ¶ A broad classification of rocks according to their origins has come into general use. The three major divisions, each with subdivisions, are *igneous, sedimentary,* and *metamorphic,* although there are overlaps among them. Igneous rocks form from molten material deep within the earth. When molten rock surges out onto the surface through volcanism, it produces extrusive rock. Should it cool and harden before reaching the earth's surface it produces intrusive rock. Crystal grains of the minerals in igneous rocks will be large if they cool slowly, small if they cool quickly. Granites with their granular textures are typical intrusive rocks, while basalts and lavas are typical noncrystalline extrusive rocks. ¶ Sedimentary rocks result from the break-up or dissolving of rocks already formed. The fragments and solutions are carried off to deposit sediments. These sediments are formed again into rock when they are compacted or cemented together by solutions of other minerals. Metamorphic rocks are also formed from other rocks already established. A change in the conditions under which a rock originally formed may force it to metamorphose into a new kind of rock. Heat and hot solutions from the intrusion of new molten material, as well as intense heat and pressure developed by bending, buckling, cracking, and shifting of the earth's crust, are typical agents of metamorphism. ¶ To study rocks, the petrographer often prepares "thin sections." A thin section is a slice of rock mounted on a glass slide. It is ground down to a thickness of about three-hundredths of a millimeter and is so thin that the several minerals in the rock will permit light to pass through. Under a special polarizing microscope the minerals can be readily studied and identified. This is the first step toward understanding what a rock is and how it formed.

PART 2: COLLECTING

An unassorted, disarranged, unlabeled pile of pebbles is not a "collection." It is merely gravel. A good collection does not just "happen," and it never forms rapidly. It is made up of properly-cared-for specimens, the best you can possibly obtain.

In the first flush of excitement, a new collector has an overpowering urge to get out in the field and collect *any* specimens he can get. The first trip may result in enough rocks to start a rock garden and even a few good study pieces, but very likely there will be nothing of quality, of serious scientific interest, well crystallized or showy. However, with persistence and good planning, the collector's prospects should gradually improve with each field excursion.

Minerals can be found almost anywhere that an opening has been made in the earth by man or nature. Excavations for roads, factories, airports, subways, and dams are all possible sources, as are operating quarries and mines. Mines usually have dump piles where worthwhile digging can be done, whether the mine is operating or not. Heavily eroded river and stream banks and the rocks of stream beds may be worth looking at. Many stream beds will even yield a little gold after considerable working of the sands and fine gravels with a prospector's gold pan or a large metal pie plate. Certain streams in southeastern Pennsylvania yield tiny brilliant chromite crystals weathered out of local serpentine rocks. Every region on earth will yield its mineralogical treasures to an ingenious and persistent collector.

Once a number of specimens has been acquired and duplicates have made their way into the collection, there is another avenue open for acquiring new specimens: exchange with other collectors. Unfortunately, most exchanges are disappointing because collectors tend to overvalue their own specimens.

One of the best rules for any exchange is that "quality brings quality." If you offer high-quality specimens, you can reasonably expect the same in return. The best procedure is to have all the ground rules of an exchange worked out beforehand. Both collectors should feel free to insist on a return of specimens if the exchange proves unsatisfactory to either. Exchanging with another collector on the spot is always better than long-distance exchanges through the mails. Needless to say, any specimens sent through the mails must be very well packed. Like gambling, exchanging can be profitable; but, just as gambling is hardly the best way to make a living, exchanging is only one way to add to a collection.

For a showy collection of classics, such as those pictured in this book, self-collected specimens will not suffice. The collector must usually turn to dealers for assistance. Recent estimates suggest that there are as many as three thousand dealers in specimens of rocks, minerals, and gems for hobbyists in the United States. Of course, there are many dealers in the rest of the world, but they are far fewer and well scattered. Nevertheless, dealers are a most important link in the specimen supply chain. Through this worldwide network of dealers the flow of new and interesting specimens is maintained for all collectors. In a hobby like this one, where each specimen is unique and there is a perpetual shortage of new and good material, the prices of specimens seem to be in a constant state of fluctuation. As with all collectible objects there, too, is a steady drift of prices upward as more people compete for too few specimens. Even with these price-inflating forces, minerals —except for those specimens of unique quality—are priced much more reasonably than are paintings, books, china, silver, and items of pottery, and other objects. Good specimens can be had for from fifty cents to $5,000, but the bulk of specimens sold to mineral collectors fall between $2 and $100. In this range the most expensive specimen is not necessarily the best. It may be rarer, but a $2 specimen may also be handsome and perfect in every way.

The specimen a collector decides to buy must meet his requirements of taste and cost. Even so, there are certain objective guidelines that will help him to invest wisely. With training and experience these guidelines can be applied rapidly and profitably. Chief among the factors affecting the price are: the specimen's intrinsic worth, if any; the kind of occurrence it represents; its size, condition, and beauty; the durability of the species; any unusual characteristics; the presence of associated species; rarity; and current market appraisal. Whether bought, collected in the field, or acquired by exchange, the same criteria will apply to the evaluation of any quality specimen added to a collection.

INTRINSIC VALUE: Certain mineral species, because of their value for other purposes, tend to bring higher prices. The gem minerals, such as topaz, tourmaline, beryl, diamond, and others, may have a much higher value than expected because they represent gem-cutting material which is valued by the carat. Even gold, silver, and platinum, and any of their family of minerals—such as the silver minerals argentite, pyrargyrite, and the proustite—tend to have higher values because of their precious-metal content. Of course, any cut and polished specimens, carvings, spheres, and other lapidary objects will carry an extra price load because of the labor and materials expended in processing them and because some are valued as art objects rather than cut mineral material.

KIND OF OCCURRENCE: Extra value is usually given if the species is an unusual occurrence for the mine or deposit from which it came. If the kinds of crystals are of unusual form for that species, or perhaps larger than most of its kind, they are generally considered more desirable. Also, crystals still attached to the rock matrix on which they formed are in greater demand. This factor is strong enough to support a thriving business in gluing loose crystals to rock or otherwise assembling them. This operation is quite different from legitimate specimen repair or restoration, and the buyer must be constantly alert for such "manufactured" specimens. When crystals do occur properly attached to their matrix, it is desirable to have them attractively arranged relative to each other, rather than just haphazardly scattered.

CONDITION: A damaged specimen is in much the same position in the mineral-specimen market as a piece of reject clothing in a clearance sale. Obvious flaws, which in minerals are chips, breaks, scratches, and discolorations, affect prices drastically. So do lack of luster, bleached-out color, and rough or etched crystal surfaces. These all indicate either deleterious weathering or poor handling and cleaning methods. Unless it is essential to their preservation, specimens which have obviously been coated with plastic sprays or dyed to improve their color are poor purchases. Those that have been pruned and trimmed so they look artificial are in the same category. Even so, judgment must be used so that excellent specimens are not rejected because they show minor damage and unobtrusive signs of having been through trimming and cleaning procedures.

BEAUTY: As in every aesthetic pursuit, beauty is

difficult to define, and there will be no attempt to define it here. Beauty in flowers, people, automobiles, dogs, and buildings is described differently for each, and so with minerals. A new collector with a high aesthetic sense can very quickly appreciate beauty in mineral specimens by viewing a large number that has been classed as beautiful by experienced collectors. Perhaps the only way to become a good judge of mineral-specimen beauty is through exposure to many of the best. Private display collections and museums with large exhibits can be very helpful.

DURABILITY: Unfortunately, there are some rather interesting and attractive mineral species that tend to be chemically unstable once they have been removed from the earth where they formed. Certain of the sulfates and borates will become opaque or actually decompose and fall apart unless extraordinary steps are taken to preserve them. Vivianite, an iron phosphate, is an example of a mineral that is popular with collectors and quite stable in collections in all climates. However, a few years ago a quantity of enormous vivianite crystals was found in the Cameroons. Through exchange the crystals were distributed around the globe. Almost all, because no special care was given to them, have since disintegrated into small pieces.

SIZE: Except in regard to the more limited appeal of very large and very small specimens, the size of a specimen has little direct relation to its price. A large but good specimen may be a world apart in price from a large but poor one. A smaller, hand-sized specimen can easily be worth more than one too big to carry. However, if it is quite large and quite good the collector who wants it is likely to find himself in competition with public and private museums. If it is average to small in size, from 6 inches down to 1 inch, and very good, then the collector will find himself in competition with all other collectors and museums, too.

UNUSUAL CHARACTERISTICS: Let us suppose that a mineral dealer has just acquired a large lot of gypsum crystals from Chihuahua, Mexico. The pieces in the lot will vary considerably in condition, quality, and size. Eventually, he has them all sorted and graded and priced. Suddenly he notices one very nice gypsum crystal that has an internal cavity. A bubble moves back and forth in the liquid-filled cavity as the specimen is tilted. Immediately, this specimen, because of a unique feature, goes into the group of more expensive specimens. Bubbles, strong or unusual color zoning or odd color combinations in otherwise ordinary crystals, naturally curved or bent crystals, peculiar iridescence or other light effects, well-developed twin crystals, and all sorts of other natural "accidents" can add to the value of a specimen. In general, however, unusual characteristics alone will not make the difference if the specimen is of poor quality.

ASSOCIATED MINERALS: When one mineral species is present on a specimen and another forms a coating on it, or a dull and uninteresting background, the result for the appeal and value of the specimen can be disastrous. Even if the two associated species are good, by competing with each other for attention their overall effect may be bad. Often, however, the two or more associated species complement each other, producing highly aesthetic contrasts in color and texture. Light yellow-green adamite on a rich red-brown limonite background, or shiny dark-blue azurite crystals partially embedded in a turbulent-looking mass of strong blue-green malachite, can be very striking—and rather expensive.

For the student of minerals, for whom aesthetics is not the prime reason for collecting, associated species can be fascinating because they tell a chemical story of the origin and development of the deposit from which the piece came. The association itself is one more clue as to what processes nature used to produce the specimen. Such a collector will value this specimen more highly than he would if it were a fine example of a single mineral species.

RARITY: Among postage stamps rarity is easily defined as a shortage of one issue or another. However, for mineral specimens, rarity is not so easy to define, even though it does drive up values as it does for postage stamps. Of course, there is a real rarity or shortage of certain species. For example, there are perhaps only a half-dozen specimens of taafeite known. For minerals, there is also the rarity of aesthetics. Out of thousands of specimens of calcite from a particular discovery perhaps only ten may be so beautiful as to raise their heads above the lot. Also, putting together all the desirable qualities of aesthetics, perfection of condition, unusual characteristics, associated minerals, etc., it is a rare specimen that meets them all to any appreciable degree. This is often spoken of as the rarity of quality.

MARKET APPRAISAL: One of the more unpredictable characteristics of the mineral-specimen market is the availability of good specimens. Sometimes there are few to be had. At other times they appear in great quantities. There have been times when every dealer in the world seemingly has gotten a stock of excellent groups of blocky, orange wulfenite crystals from Chihuahua, Mexico. At such times the price schedule seems to weaken, and the specimens are less expensive. A few months later, with the wulfenite stock well on its way to absorption by the market, the prices swing up again. An astute collector will keep in touch with the specimen market, as one might the stock market, to know whether the price of the specimen he wants is reasonable, considering the state of the market. In practice, he will probably buy it anyway, knowing that later it may be gone.

Handling Specimens

Even to the neophyte it soon becomes obvious that any mineral specimen deserves careful handling. Although some may seem heavy and hard, almost all specimens can be damaged so easily that they must be handled more carefully than fine china. Some are actually so delicate that they should not be handled at all except in moments of absolute necessity. There are even some which are chemically marred by skin acids if moist fingers touch splendent crystal faces. This doesn't mean that specimens shouldn't be touched at all after they are removed from the earth. Quite the contrary. Every specimen, whether fresh-dug from a mine or brought home in a dealer's cotton-lined box, probably needs cleaning. Specimens that are not soluble in water or not decomposed by it are washed with a soft brush and a little detergent; soap is not used because it may leave a dulling film when it dries. Clay or loose dirt will often be found stuck in small crevices and cavities, but a dental probe or even a toothpick can loosen it enough to be scrubbed off with an old toothbrush under a stream of water. A brush is out of the question, of course, for very fragile crystals. These can be dunked a few times in detergent wash water or kept immersed in the water while a strong current is directed at them with a syringe. Specimens, like halite, that are soluble in water or, like marcasite, that may eventually decompose if not thoroughly dried may be washed in alcohol and then set in a warm spot to dry. Fibrous and hairy specimens that may mat down when wet can be dusted by blowing a current of air over them.

Frequently, cleaning methods must be a little more rigorous. Iron stains or coatings of minerals like calcite and quartz must be removed if the specimen is to appear in its maximum glory. A water solution of hydrochloric (muriatic) acid will often remove iron stains and will readily dissolve calcite coatings. If the desirable part of the specimen is also soluble in acids, then acids must be avoided, of course. A solution of oxalic acid, a white crystalline powder, in water also makes an excellent iron-stain remover, especially when warmed. Since oxalic acid is poisonous, due precaution must be taken. Quartz coatings are more difficult to remove. They can be taken off by soaking the specimen in hydrofluoric acid. This is a messy process, since the fumes will etch porcelain and glass, and must be done in plastic containers out-of-doors. The art of specimen cleaning has been developed by collectors over a period of time, and all sorts of chemical solvents are used for specific purposes. For example, liquid dip-type cleaners normally used for polishing the family silver will work as well for some silver minerals. There are even collectors who believe that pyrite and marcasite suffer decomposition because of bacterial attack and dip their specimens in antibiotics as a preventive measure.

Cleaning alone may not bring out the potential of some good specimens. Surgery may also be necessary. Carefully trimming away unnecessary rock and broken material may produce a final product that is quite pleasing—an expression of your own tastes. The trick is to avoid ruining the specimen by breaking or bruising it in the wrong place. Even then, all is not lost. Bruises can be carefully smoothed with fine emery paper and touched with glycerine or clear epoxy cement. If adhesives are needed for more serious repairs they should be used with restraint and should be clear and colorless. Epoxy cements take some time to dry but give stronger bonding to pieces you may be reassembling like a jigsaw puzzle. If an assembled specimen looks obviously repaired it should be disposed of as a surgical failure. Trimming of mineral specimens can be done with a hammer and chisel, but this causes considerable shock and can be disastrous. Regular, commercially available mineral trimmers are worth the cost.

Now and then a specimen is acquired that needs to be given a flat and polished surface before it shows its internal patterns, colors, or inclusions of impurities to best advantage. Golden rutile needles embedded in glassy quartz, the striking color patterns of Mexican agates, the concentric bull's-eye patterns of green malachite, and many other similarly exotic effects never show well except with polished surfaces. Such cutting and polishing can be done commercially or by amateurs who have their own cutting equipment.

Once a specimen is properly trimmed and cleaned, it is ready to be put in a convenient but safe place. There is no point in acquiring, cleaning, and otherwise preparing a fine specimen unless a good attempt is made to preserve it in the peak of its condition. Lighted glass cases and dust-proof drawers are best for a collection containing numerous specimens. However, lighted shadow boxes and any other display techniques that serve well for sculptures, china, glass, and other art objects are also good for minerals. Fortunately, if the home you have given a specimen, perhaps as part of the décor of a room, does not protect it from dust and grime, the specimen can always be washed again.

Under any conditions of storage and use, the identity of the specimen and the locality from which it came must be preserved, otherwise its scientific and market value is drastically reduced. Labels are usually the answer. In collections of only a few specimens, the labels can be tucked away in some convenient spot. Serious collectors with many specimens face the problem of keeping track of too many labels and the possibility of a specimen and its label becoming separated. Applying a small number to the back of the specimen and matching it with a number on the label is the simple solution. Some camera enthusiasts maintain photographic records of their collections.

Building an Interest

There are two major ways to build an interest in any collecting hobby. It is essential, first, to acquire at least a few specimens and, second, to see as many good specimens as possible. Ways to acquire specimens have already been reviewed. There are three obvious settings in which to view collections of good specimens. Most numerous, perhaps, are the homes of private collectors, who are usually delighted to show their acquisitions. One of the easiest ways to meet other collectors is to join, or at least visit, a local mineral society, of which there are hundreds. Most of the large number of clubs and societies in the United States and some in other countries are listed each April in the *Lapidary Journal,* one of the major magazines of the hobby. There are other good magazines to keep you abreast of collecting activities, the best of which is the *Mineralogical Record.*

The second place to see good specimens is mineral shows. There are hundreds of these shows held each year. Usually, they are operated by local societies, although there are regional and even national shows and a couple of commercially run shows. Certain of the shows, such as the Zurich Show and the Altdorf Show in Europe, and the Tucson, Pasadena, and Detroit shows in the United States, are internationally recognized for their importance and for the superb minerals normally seen there. Members and officers of the local clubs and societies, as well as the hobby magazines, are good sources of information about show dates and places.

The third and best place to see good specimens is in a museum. The quality of a museum exhibit depends not only on the quality of its collections. Other factors are the money available for exhibit preparation and the caliber of the staff that plans and prepares exhibits. Most mineral museums lack either quality collections, trained exhibit staff, or money. Even so, they manage to show the public a wide variety of good specimens. Most museums have collected their minerals over many generations. They improve their collections through gifts and bequests, by field work and exchange activities of curators, and even by purchases. Thus they preserve fine specimens from the past for future generations to see.

Many of the large cities of the world have fascinating museum collections—some originating as parts of royal collections of former times. In Europe the greatest of all is the collection in the British

Museum of Natural History. In the United States the Smithsonian Institution collection is of similar excellence. These two and perhaps another half-dozen important collections in the world are wondrous sights to behold, even for an experienced collector. True to their trust, these few museums present to the mineral-specimen connoisseur a vast array of specimens illustrating all the variety and perfection possible in the mineral kingdom.

A serious collector will want to return to a mineral museum as often as possible, to browse slowly through the exhibit and see many things that the casual viewer misses. Much can be learned in this way about what makes a good-quality specimen. Labels also give information about mineral localities. Excellent crystals of many species will help the student of crystallography. Minerals commonly associated with each other, normal color for the species, the kinds of deposits in which minerals occur, comparisons of the same species from different localities, and many other bits of mineral information can be discovered in the exhibits. Perhaps even more important, a visit to a museum mineral collection is usually a very pleasant aesthetic experience. Beautiful and interesting specimens whet the collector's appetite to raise the quality of his collection.

Mineral Study

People may differ in being tall and short, fat and thin, witty and dull. Just so, mineral species are recognized and differentiated from each other by certain sets of characteristics. Scientists have worked for more than two hundred years to bring knowledge about mineral characteristics from chaos to order. In the process a set of criteria has been established to best separate and group the various species and families of minerals. The first serious attempt at doing this was made by Abraham Gottlieb Werner, professor of mineralogy at Freiburg, Saxony. In 1774, two years before the American Revolution, he published an essay on the "External Characters of Minerals." His ideas caught on and spread rapidly over Europe and the rest of the educated world. It then became much easier to see the relationships among minerals and to base predictions about their chemical and physical behavior on these relationships.

At about this same time, René Just Haüy, professor of mineralogy at the Museum of Natural History in Paris and honorary canon of the cathedral of Nôtre Dame, was laying the firm foundation for what was to become the science of crystallography. Through it, an understanding of one of the most fundamental differences among mineral species was given to us. The internal structure of minerals is now well understood. It only remained for the Swedish chemist Jöns Jakob Berzelius, by the start of the nineteenth century, to show that mineral species could be differentiated and organized by their chemical composition. Of course, all three of these men— Werner, Haüy, and Berzelius—were using information and theories that had been painstakingly and laboriously developed by others. It was their task to discover the underlying meanings. Then, too, hundreds since them have labored to find proofs, to refine and expand the basic ideas, and to apply them.

Today the professional mineralogist relies on chemical and crystallographic characteristics to name and classify mineral species. This kind of classification scheme was not really well established until 1884, when James Dwight Dana, professor of mineralogy at Yale, published his *System of Mineralogy*. At first his "System," although including crystallography, was almost totally a chemical classification. In 1885 X-rays were discovered, and by 1912 their application to minerals proved the key to understanding crystal structures. Classification systems since that time, including subsequent modernizations of Dana's System, have been based on a combination of the chemical and crystallographic characteristics of minerals.

It is surprising, with all this scientific development of mineral knowledge, that in many cases, and certainly for amateur collectors, Werner's original approach still holds good. Most common minerals, at least, are distinguished from each other by simple external characteristics. Nothing is quite so satisfactory for a mineral collector, using this idea, as to be able to pick up a specimen and identify it by sight in a matter of seconds. There are some people who seem to be able to do this so effortlessly that it suggests magic or at least extrasensory perception. The fact is that there is no easy way to acquire the skill. It comes from long periods of study of external mineral characteristics, coupled with a good memory.

Physical Characteristics

The hallmarks by which minerals can be recognized and differentiated may be divided for convenience into two groups: physical and chemical characteristics. Some of the physical characteristics require elaborate laboratory equipment for measurement. Those physical characteristics to be emphasized here are chosen for their usefulness to the amateur collector. He alone can later determine their order of importance for his own purposes and which of them he can use, considering the limitations of his testing equipment. Hardness, tenacity, cleavage, growth pattern, luster, diaphaneity, streak, fluorescence, magnetism, and crystal habit are sufficient checks for performing many mineral identifications.

HARDNESS: This has been very reasonably defined as the degree of resistance to scratching. Like most physical characteristics of minerals, this one depends on the mineral's structure or the way in which the atoms composing it are hooked together. Those with atoms tightly bound will resist the loss of small bits and chips—or being scratched—when rubbed against something else. In the early 1800's the German mineralogist Friedrich Mohs proposed a scale of mineral hardness which, while not very good, has proved useful and practical ever since. In this scale, ten well-known minerals were selected to represent various degrees of hardness. Talc, one of the softest known, and diamond, the hardest known, were selected for the ends of the scale, and the others ranked between. In order they are: talc (1), gypsum (2), calcite (3), fluorite (4), apatite (5), feldspar (6), quartz (7), topaz (8), corundum (9), and diamond (10). The weakness of the Mohs scale lies in the fact that hardness differences are not uniform. For example, there is almost as much of a hardness difference between #9 and #10 as there is between #1 and #9.

Minerals in the scale are used for attempting to scratch an unknown specimen. If, say, a small piece of feldspar (#6) will not scratch the unknown, but topaz (#8) will, the hardness of the specimen will be somewhere between 6 and 8. If a piece of quartz (#7) also scratches, the hardness of the unknown must then be 6.5, or at least somewhere between 6 and 7. It is best to try scratching a fresh surface, since exposed surfaces are frequently altered by nature to something else. Also, care should be taken to wipe off the

154

powder from the tiny scratch to see that a true scratch mark has been left and not just a powdered trail from the hardness-testing mineral itself.

Of course, a choice mineral specimen or a gem can be disastrously marred by scratching in a conspicuous place. All such operations must be carried out on a very small scale in some obscure spot. Some mineral-specimen dealers stock sets of hardness pencils. These have tiny pieces of the hardness minerals set in their ends so that carefully controlled, minute scratches can be made. If convenient, this test could even be made with the aid of a magnifying glass or a microscope, so it can be done on an even smaller scale.

TENACITY: Every prospector going west in the gold-rush days soon learned a simple test to distinguish between real gold and "fool's gold," or pyrite, each of which resembles the other. On beating a tiny grain with a hammer, real gold would flatten out into a rough plate. "Fool's gold" would shatter into a powder. This is a perfect demonstration of what is meant by tenacity—the way a mineral holds together. There is quite a difference between hardness and toughness, which is a measure of tenacity. Topaz is much harder than jade, for example. However, jade is so tough that it holds together under physical punishment while topaz shatters. It is the toughness of jade that makes it so durable for delicate carvings.

Several terms have been adopted to describe the tenacity of a mineral, and most are self-explanatory. The *brittle* nature of pyrite, which shatters when struck, has already been compared to the *malleability* of gold, which can be hammered thin. Gold, like copper and silver, is also *ductile:* it can be drawn out into thin wire. Muscovite, one of the mica family, is *elastic:* it returns to its original shape when bent. By contrast, gypsum is *flexible:* it bends, but the bend is permanent. Gypsum also happens to be *sectile,* which means that thin shavings can be pared with a knife, much like whittling a hard wood. With no tools at all, or with very simple tools, it is possible to get some idea of a mineral's tenacity from a tiny scrap removed from some inconspicuous spot.

CLEAVAGE: One would think that all breakage is the same. And yet we know that glass does not break in the same pattern as metal. Minerals, too, differ in their breakage patterns. On coming apart, some leave rough or jagged surfaces, while others leave smooth but irregular surfaces. Such breaking, without pattern, is called *fracture*. Some hematite has a habit of breaking in very flat surfaces. However, this characteristic is limited only to certain specimens of hematite from very limited deposits and is caused by peculiarities of formation which occurred in those particular deposits. This kind of geometric but unpredictable breaking is called *parting*. Still other species always break predictably along very flat surfaces in very definite directions related to their internal atomic structure. Mica is an excellent example of a species that splits so well in one direction that a single piece of any mica can be separated into numerous, thin, elastic sheets, so thin perhaps as to be almost invisible. This kind of breakage is called *cleavage*. Galena and halite (salt) cleave so easily in three perpendicular directions that it is easy to break out perfect, shiny cubes. Calcite cleaves in three directions also, but not at right angles to each other. Feldspars cleave in two directions, leaving a jagged surface when attempts are made to break them in the third direction. It is the very, very easy cleavage of graphite in one direction that makes it a good lubricant. It cleaves so easily that one layer slides freely from its attachment to another, and therefore the objects separated by a grain of graphite can only slide with the parted layers.

GROWTH PATTERN: There are many forces, both internal and in the external environment, that will have an effect on the way a mineral grows and how the finished specimen will look. The individual crystals of some minerals, and even groups of crystals, tend to form or group themselves in recognizable patterns. Crystals may be *acicular* (needle-like), or they may be *bladed,* or even *tabular,* like flat tablets. They may be *pyramidal,* looking like three-, four-, or six-sided pyramids, or capillary (hair-like). In groups they may be *arborescent* or *dendritic,* which means they are in a branching, tree-like arrangement. Some masses of closely packed crystals are *botryoidal,* that is, grape-like (from the Greek), or *mammillary* if the rounded masses are more like a breast, or even *reniform* when in roughly rounded masses like kidneys. Asbestos comes in *fibrous* masses. Aragonite is sometimes *coralloidal*—in twisted, tangled groups that look like white coral. Rutile and cerussite often are *reticulated,* occurring in open, net-like lattices made of numerous crossed bars of crystals. Dozens of other terms, such as *plumose, nodular, pisolitic, drusy, micaceous,* and *stalactitic,* are used to describe a growth pattern that is repeated often enough to help recognize minerals growing that way.

LUSTER: It is fairly easy to distinguish between a mineral that looks metallic and one that does not. In doing so, a distinction is made about its surface appearance, or luster. Of course, there are other kinds of lusters than metallic. Even the metallic-looking minerals can be subdivided into those with submetallic, white-metallic, black-metallic, yellow-metallic, and other lusters. Among the nonmetallic-looking minerals, greasy luster, pearly luster, glassy or vitreous luster, adamantine or diamond-like luster are all easy to detect with little or no training and skill. Other, more subtle, lusters, such as *resinous* and *silky,* as well as degrees of luster, such as *dull, shining, splendent,* and *glistening,* become obvious with a little experience in judging them.

DIAPHANEITY: Although this is a formidable-looking word, it merely refers to the amount of transparency a mineral sample may have. There are a number of minerals, such as magnetite, that are so extremely *opaque* that even tiny grains or splinters will not pass any visible light. Some, like neptunite, seem opaque but will transmit a little light through edges or tiny, thin pieces. Still others are *translucent,* and others are quite *transparent.* Most of the important gem minerals, such as diamond, sapphire, beryl, and tourmaline, can be transparent.

STREAK: Often the real color of a mineral shows better when it is powdered. For example, hematite specimens may sometimes appear brown or red or even black; they may be dull or highly splendent. However, all of them leave a distinctly red streak on a streak plate. Pyrite specimens almost always look bright and brassy, but the species always leaves a black streak. It is easy to find the streak of a mineral by rubbing a small fragment of it repeatedly on a piece of unglazed porcelain tile. Most porcelains have a hardness of about 7, so that if the mineral is softer it will leave several streaks of powdered material behind. For minerals harder than 7, it is a simple

156

matter to powder some with a hammer to get the same kind of diagnostic color.

FLUORESCENCE: Certain minerals, when exposed to invisible ultraviolet, or "black," light from special types of lamps, glow in beautiful colors. Ultraviolet light is much like visible light, except that our eyes are not designed to see it. Some minerals absorb this kind of light, hold it temporarily, change it into visible light of some color, and give it off again for us to see. Discovered by Sir George Stokes in 1852, this phenomenon was called fluorescence because he first measured it in the mineral fluorite.

Not all species fluoresce; some, such as calcite, may be fluorescent when found in one mine but not in another. Other species, such as scheelite, always fluoresce and always in the same color. For scheelite this can be helpful for prospecting and ore separation, since the scheelite under an ultraviolet lamp clearly stands out as a bright bluish-white against the non-fluorescent minerals associated with it. There are inexpensive ultraviolet lamps available, so that even a beginning collector can own one.

MAGNETISM: Although many mineral species are very slightly attracted by a strong magnet, the characteristic is of limited use to the collector. But when needed to distinguish magnetite, which is strongly attracted, from the lookalike species franklinite, ilmenite, or chromite, it works simply and perfectly. To distinguish pyrrhotite—the only brassy colored mineral whose small fragments are strongly attracted —from pyrite, chalcopyrite, and others that resemble it, the test for magnetism is crucial.

COLOR: Unfortunately for the collector, mineral color is not always an unvarying characteristic. Minerals can be either *idiochromatic* or *allochromatic*. Idiochromatic minerals are those whose own chemical composition and internal structure are responsible for their color. Allochromatic minerals may have variable color, depending upon their impurities. Thus, sulfur is idiochromatic and always yellow. Pyrite is brass-colored, hematite and cinnabar are red, orpiment is yellow, malachite green, and azurite blue. Beryl is allochromatic and may be colorless, green, blue, pink, red, or yellow.

Sometimes the color of a mineral has little to do with its own chemical composition or structure, or with the presence of allochromatic impurities. Opal, for example, may flash out its brilliant play of colors, caused by a process called *diffraction* and resulting from the way the opal was originally deposited and packed together from solution in beds of sediments. Diamond and a few other species exhibit strong flashes of red, yellow, blue, and other colors because of their strong *dispersion*. This means that diamond is able to separate the colors in white light, any one of which may be flashed back to the observer when he and a reflecting face of the diamond are in appropriate positions.

For the collector, then, this means that, with considerable judgment, the color of a mineral can be a guide to its identification.

SPECIFIC GRAVITY: Because of the need for a suitable apparatus and some arithmetical ability, specific-gravity tests may be more difficult than others for the amateur collector to handle. Perhaps the best way to think of the specific gravity of minerals is as a measure of their comparative weights. When you pick up a piece of topaz it seems heavy for its size.

A piece of galena of the same size seems even heavier while quartz seems lighter. Technically, this phenomenon is known as *density*—the weight of a certain volume of a substance. When we compare this weight with that of an equal volume of water, however, it is known as specific gravity. Thus, when we see that a diamond weighs three and a half times as much as the same volume of water, its specific gravity is 3.5. Galena has a specific gravity of about 7.5, topaz of 3.5, and quartz about 2.5. An adequate test for the characteristic of specific gravity is not possible without some kind of weighing equipment. Scientific supply houses advertise balances suitable for the purpose at fairly low cost; it is even possible to construct one from readily available materials.

INDEX OF REFRACTION: As with specific gravity, the determination of an index of refraction requires special equipment. *Refraction* is the ability of a substance to bend a beam of light from its original path as the light enters and leaves it. All minerals through which light can pass have different refracting abilities which depend on their structures. One of the best ways to measure this ability is by use of a small instrument called a refractometer. A small mineral fragment is placed with a bright cleavage face or a crystal face against the polished glass top of the instrument with a drop of highly refractive liquid between them to insure good contact. A light beam is passed through the instrument and reflected off the fragment back toward a viewing eyepiece. There is a scale in the eyepiece from which refractive index can be read directly. It is a rapid and accurate method for mineral identification.

X-RAY EXAMINATION: Undoubtedly, X-ray determination of mineral species is the most accurate and foolproof of all methods. However, it is best left to professional mineralogists. The cost of the equipment needed, of training the operators, and of supporting X-ray files and film-developing facilities is prohibitive. X-ray procedures for mineral identification are quite different from those used by surgeons and dentists. In the most commonly used technique, called the powder diffraction procedure, only a tiny portion of the mineral species is used and this is powdered. Films in specially constructed cameras record, as a series of curved lines, the presence of atomic planes which a beam of X-rays detects on its passage through the sample. For each species the pattern of lines is characteristic and will be different from that of other species. The films can be indexed and filed and used much the same way as fingerprints.

Even ignoring specific gravity, index of refraction, and X-ray characteristics, important as they are, the collector and connoisseur of minerals will still have a good battery of physical tests with which to develop his acquaintance with minerals.

Crystallography

Because solids, with few exceptions, have orderly internal arrangements of their atoms, they are called crystals. Fortunately, for aesthetic and scientific reasons, when crystals form under favorable conditions, they grow in very distinctive shapes. These solid shapes have their surfaces covered by flat faces in an orderly, geometrical arrangement. The kinds of faces and their arrangements depend entirely on the mineral species. This means that a knowledge of possible faces is a powerful tool for studying the species.

The study of crystal faces and their meanings

is called crystal morphology and it is an art and science that modern crystallographers have generally forsaken for the better X-ray methods. However, in years past, a well-organized science of crystal morphology was developed. All crystals, it had been discovered, can conveniently and logically be divided into thirty-two different kinds of groups, or crystal classes, depending on the symmetry of arrangement of the crystal faces. For further convenience and simplification, the thirty-two classes can be grouped into six crystal systems. All the classes in any one system have some important symmetry in common and they are the only classes that have it. The systems are called the isometric, tetragonal, orthorhombic, monoclinic, triclinic, and hexagonal. The crystals belonging in the isometric system show the highest amount of symmetry and those in the triclinic system the lowest.

Everyone recognizes a cube. It is one of the high-symmetry forms belonging in the isometric system. A good beginning book in morphological crystallography, a set of simple crystal models, and some long evenings will add rapidly to the list of forms—octahedron, dodecahedron, prism, pinacoid, pyramid, and many others—that a collector can recognize as belonging to one crystal system or another.

Natural crystals, unlike models, tend to be confusing because sometimes all the faces of a form are not present. The crystals may be partially broken. Some of the faces may be buried in the matrix, and to remove a crystal for examination might ruin a specimen. Nature hinders identification by producing a deformed crystal with faces in the correct places at the correct angles to each other, but some too big and some too small. Then, too, natural crystals rarely show only one form. They tend to

be present in combinations on a single crystal. One of the more difficult situations arises when a crystal of a mineral species has been replaced chemically by another species without changing its outer shape. Such an object is called a *pseudomorph* (false shape). In such cases only experience with crystals will provide the necessary clues to solve the problem. Of course, a knowledge of crystallography is not necessary for assembling a good suite of specimens. However, it is one of those related studies that increase knowledge of minerals and add to the pleasures of collecting them. No equipment is required except a book, and the study is especially appealing to those who find pleasure in mental activity which requires no previous background knowledge.

Chemical Mineralogy

Minerals are naturally-occurring chemical substances. They differ, however, in various ways from the manufactured chemicals found in a laboratory. Naturally occurring minerals may exist in large-sized crystals, with variable amounts of impurities, and somewhat variable compositions, while those in the laboratory tend to be much purer and are usually stored in powder form or in some finely divided state. A laboratory chemical, on the other hand, will have the same characteristics as a sample of the same chemical from any other laboratory. As an example of the difference, the black lead sulfide used by the chemist is the same thing chemically as the mineral galena found in a lead mine, but the natural galena very likely is in large, silvery crystals and may have impurities of silver, zinc, or even gold.

All matter found on the earth, including man himself, is composed of about a hundred basic substances called elements. The elements are united in various proportions with each other to form great numbers of different combinations. Of all these elements, only twenty make up 99.5 percent of the earth's crust. Of these twenty just about eight comprise 97 percent of the earth's rocks and minerals. As every mineral species in turn is described by mineralogists, the chemical composition is carefully determined. With the composition known, the species can be classified in a list with its nearest relatives. Of the various classifications, perhaps the best known is the Dana System mentioned earlier. Begun in the 1800's by James D. Dana and Edward S. Dana, this system arranges the species from the simplest chemical compositions to the most complex. The major groupings of the Dana System, with a mineral example of each, are as follows:

GROUP	TYPICAL MINERAL	ELEMENT CONTENTS
Native elements	diamond	carbon
Sulfides, selenides, tellurides	pyrite	iron, sulfur
Sulfosalts	enargite	copper, arsenic, sulfur
Oxides	anatase	titanium, oxygen
Halides	fluorite	calcium, fluorine
Carbonates	calcite	calcium, carbon, oxygen
Nitrates	niter	potassium, nitrogen, oxygen
Iodates	salesite	copper, iodine, oxygen
Borates	borax	sodium, boron, oxygen, hydrogen
Sulfates	anglesite	lead, sulfur, oxygen
Selenates, tellurates	mackayite	iron, tellurium, oxygen, hydrogen
Chromates	crocoite	lead, chromium, oxygen
Phosphates, arsenates, vanadates	vivianite	iron, phosphorus, oxygen, hydrogen
Antimonates	nadorite	lead, antimony, oxygen, chlorine
Molybdates, tungstates	scheelite	calcium, tungsten, oxygen
Organic compounds	whewellite	calcium, carbon, oxygen, hydrogen

It is true that some training in chemistry is crucial in mastering the chemical identification of minerals. There are a number of tests directed toward the purpose that are particularly useful to anyone with this training. The old classic book on blowpipe analysis by J. G. Brush, with mineral tables by S. L. Penfield, is perhaps still the best. *Qualitative Chemical Analysis and Identification of Minerals* by Orsino Smith also has excellent mineral-chemistry tables.

Without technical education or elaborate equipment, a collector still has at hand a number of simple chemical tests he can use. Many so-called "spot tests" can be easily applied. Whether or not a tiny fragment of the mineral will dissolve readily in water or acid can be determined by anyone. Whether or not a small fragment effervesces, or bubbles, when acid is applied is an obvious test and a useful one for determining the presence of carbonate minerals. By leafing through some of the books on chemical spot tests or blowpipe analysis over a period of time, a card file of "recipes" can be assembled. The collector does not need to know why the tests work so long as he knows how to interpret them.

Now, armed with some historical perspective, an insight into the chemical and physical nature of minerals, and enthusiasm about the aesthetic and scientific satisfactions to be derived from mineral collecting, you are ready to join the search for buried treasure. You will soon be seen browsing around mineral dealer's displays, wandering in and out of their shops, visiting auction houses, antique and second-hand furniture shops, other collections, museums, mines, quarries, excavations, and any other places that show or supply specimens. You will be engaged in a fascinating cultural activity while you increase your knowledge of the mineral kingdom.